SILENCE

by
Nicola Werenowska

A Mercury Theatre Colchester, Wiltshire Creative and Unity
Theatre Liverpool Production

Published by Playdead Press 2018

© Nicola Werenowska 2018

Nicola Werenowska has asserted her rights under the
Copyright, Design and Patents Act, 1988, to be
identified as the authors of this work.

A CIP catalogue record for this book is available from
the British Library.

ISBN 978-1-910067-71-0

Playdead Press
www.playdeadpress.com

SILENCE

by Nicola Werenowska

CAST

MARIA	**Tina Gray**
EWA	**Kate Spiro**
ANNA	**Maria Louis**

CREATIVE

Director	**Jo Newman**
Designer	**Baśka Wesołowska**
Lighting Designer	**Zoe Spurr**
Composition & Sound Designer	**Helen Skiera**
Composition & Sound Designer	**Bethany Duke**
Producer	**Dilek Latif**
Dialect Coach	**Karina Knapinska**

SILENCE has been funded by Arts Council England, the Mercury Theatre Colchester, Unity Theatre Liverpool, and Wiltshire Creative, and developed in association with the Mercury Theatre, Lakeside Theatre, Essex Book Festival.

After sharings at the Mercury Theatre and the Arts Theatre, Nov 2016, *SILENCE* received its first performance at the Mercury Theatre, Colchester on 12 October 2018 before touring nationally.

CAST

TINA GRAY | MARIA

Training: Royal Academy of Music. Drama Dept. 1958-61

Theatre: *Talking Heads – Soldiering On* (Leeds Playhouse); *Murder, Margaret And Me, The Importance of Being Earnest* (Salisbury Playhouse); *Tartuffe* (Tobacco Factory, Bristol); *Damned Rebel Bitches* (Poorboy, Scotland Tour); *Steel Magnolias, Don't Look Now* (Hornchurch); *The Singing Stones* (Arcola); *The History Boys* (National Theatre); *The Ghost Train* (Brockley Jack); *To Kill a Mockingbird, Habeus Corpus, Enjoy, Pygmalion, Noises Off* (York Theatre Royal); *A Passionate Woman* (Keswick); *Endgame, The White Devil* (Liverpool Everyman); *On Golden Pond, A Woman of No Importance, Flamingoland, Perfect Days* (New Vic); *The Glass Menagerie, Tess of the D'Urbervilles, Martin Chuzzlwit* (Coventry); *Relative Values* (Theatre Royal, Bath & Tour); *Our Ellen* (Ongoing one woman play, written for Tina by Richard Osborne); 13 Panto Fairies, across the land, a particular favourite being Fairy Grizelda in *Babes In The Wood* at Colchester Mercury.

Television includes: *The Last Kingdom; Scott and Bailey; Doctors; Heartbeat; Coronation Street.*

Film includes: *Agatha Christie's The Crooked House; The Decoy Bride; Above The Clouds; Arifa; Angels in Notting Hill; Streets in the Sky* and 5 Rosamund Pilchers for German TV.

Radio includes: Over 1,500 Radio plays and readings for the BBC including *The Archers, The Vicar of Wakefield, The Piano, Mill on the Floss, Persuasion* and *Murder at the Vicarage.* Member of the BBC Radio Drama Company 1993-4.

KATE SPIRO | EWA

Kate trained with the National Youth Theatre of GB and subsequently at Bristol Old Vic Theatre School over 35 years ago.

TV: *Oedipus At Colonus*; *Iphegenia At Aulis*; *EastEnders*; *Brookside*; *To Be The Best*; *Natural Lies*; *The Bill*; *An Ungentlemanly Act*; *Down To Earth*; *Holby City*; *Hollyoaks*; *Doctors*; *Brexit.*

Film: *An Ungentlemanly Act*; *Brexit* and Film Shorts including *Dignity*; *The Farm*; *I Wouldn't Wish The Eighties On Anyone.*

Theatre: *Outside Edge, Cider with Rosie, The Dresser* (Cheltenham Everyman); *Good* (RSC for Aldwych theatre & Broadway); *The Gaps in Augustus* (Orchard Theatre); *Time and Time Again* (Edinburgh); *Twelfth Night* (Plymouth Theatre Royal); *Hard Times, Diary Of A Scoundrel, Hamlet, The First Quarto* (Orange Tree Theatre); *Bedroom Farce* (Exeter Northcott); *Les Liaisons Dangereuses* (RSC for Ambassadors Theatre); *Lorca's Women* (RSC Barbican platform); *The Shaughraun, Bartholomew Fair* (Olivier, National Theatre); *The Doll's House* (Basingstoke Haymarket); *The Silver King* (Chichester Festival); *Hobson's Choice* (Derby Playhouse); *Murder in Green Meadows, Building Blocks* (Nuffield Theatre); *Frobishers Gold, Hotbed Shorts* (Menagerie, Cambridge & Theatre 503); *The Glass Menagerie* (New Wolsey, Ipswich).

Kate has recently finished filming alongside Benedict Cumberbatch on James Graham's forthcoming film for Channel 4 with the working title *Brexit*.

MARIA LOUIS | ANNA

Maria trained at ALRA.

Theatre credits include: *A Streetcar Named Desire* (English Touring Theatre / NST / Theatre Clwyd); *Chicken Palace* (Theatre Royal Stratford East); *Low Level Panic* (The Albany / StoneCrabs Theatre Company) and *Selfie Rules* (Team Angelica / Theatre Royal Stratford East).

Television credits include: *Kiss of Death* (October Films / Talos Films), *Coconut* (BBC3), *People Just Do Nothing* (Series 1 & 2 BBC) and *Doctors* (BBC).

Feature Film credits include: *Six from Eight* (6 from 8 Productions) and *Follow Me* (Samurai Films).

CREATIVE TEAM

JO NEWMAN | Director

Jo is associate director at Wiltshire Creative (Salisbury Playhouse, Salisbury Arts Centre and Salisbury International Arts Festival). She was awarded a Regional Theatre Young Director's Scheme 18 month residency at Salisbury Playhouse (2015-16) and was previously Co-Artistic Director of Tin Box Theatre Company and part of the team managing PILOT Nights, Birmingham.

Training: University of Birmingham (BA Hons Drama and Theatre Arts and MPhil B Directing and Dramaturgy)

Directing Credits Include: *A Wiltshire Tale* (Salisbury Arts Centre & Tour); *Hansel* (Salisbury Playhouse); *Happiness Ltd* (Bike Shed, Theatre Royal Plymouth, Salisbury Playhouse & Tour); *Betrayal* (Salisbury Playhouse); *This Land* (Pentabus,

Salisbury Playhouse & Tour); *Pint Dreams* (Tin Box Theatre, Holding space commission & UK tour); *Not Known at This Address* (Tin Box Theatre, UK tour); *Stop the Clocks* (Tin Box Theatre, The Coffin Works).

As assistant director: *The Magna Carta Plays, Bike, Fallen Angels* (Salisbury Playhouse); *Little Shop of Horrors* (Salisbury Playhouse & Mercury Theatre Colchester); *The Palace of Wasted Dreams* (mac Birmingham).

Jo was Associate Director on *we're here because we're here* (National Theatre, Jeremy Deller, 14-18 Now) and conducted verbatim interviews for *My Country* (National Theatre).

NICOLA WERENOWSKA | Writer

After a flirtation with playwriting when she was 16 (her play *20%* was runner-up in 1988 Royal Court Young Playwrights' Competition), Nicola began playwriting in 2003, following her dyspraxia diagnosis.

Productions include: *CASH!, Davy's Day* (Mercury Theatre); *Peapickers*, Guesthouse (Eastern Angles); *Freedoms of the Forest* (Menagerie); *BirthDate* (Nabakov); *Tu I Teraz* (Hampstead Theatre, Nuffield Theatre, Mercury Theatre); *Tattooed Under Your Skin* (Theatre 503); *Hidden* (Oxford Playhouse, Marlowe Theatre, Mercury Theatre).

Her work has been longlisted for national competitions, (Verity Bargate, Bruntwood, PapaTango) and *Hidden* was runner up for the Mercury Prize 2016.

Nicola has been on attachment to Graeae, a member of the Royal Court National group and is playwright in residence at Lakeside Theatre. She currently has work in development with the New Wolsey Theatre, Graeae, and the Marlowe Theatre and is co-writer for BBC Radio 4's adaptation of *Little Dorrit* for the 2018/19 Christmas period.

BAŚKA WESOŁOWSKA | Designer

Baśka is a young Polish artist who graduated from the Theatre Design postgraduate course at the Royal Academy of Dramatic Art. Before coming to London she had previously graduated from the Academy of Fine Arts in Katowice with a Master's Degree in Painting in 2013.

Baśka has previously designed several productions in her home country of Poland. She has a wide experience working on both fringe/immersive theatre and for large-scale venues. However, what matters to her the most is the story. She enjoys finding a unique aesthetic language and combing art with theatre design.

Her most recent London credits include: *Greek* (Grimeborn Festival at Arcola Theatre); *Ladykiller* (Edinburgh Festival, Pleasance Theatre); *Anna-Liisa* (RADA Festival); *Touching Home* (Deli Theatre); *Coconut* (Ovalhouse Theatre); *Cause* (Vaults Festival); *Doodle* (Waterloo East Theatre); *Strange Orchestra* (Vanbrugh Theatre, RADA) *The House of Bernarda Alba, Clay to Flesh, Loveplay* (GBS Theatre, RADA).

HELEN SKIERA | Composer & Sound Designer

The Lovely Bones (Royal and Derngate and Tour); *This is Not for You* (Graeae GDIF and SIRF); *Instructions for Correct Assembly, Bodies* (Royal Court Theatre); *Betrayal, Echo's End, The Magna Carta Plays* (Salisbury Playhouse); *The Encounter* (Complicite); *Crossings, Here I Belong* (Pentabus); *Good Dog, I Know All the Secrets in My World, The Epic Adventure of Nhamo* the *Manyika Warrior and his Sexy Wife Chipo, The Legend of Hamba* (Tiata Fahodzi); *House and Garden* (Watermill); *Harajuku Girls* (Finborough Theatre); *The Dog, The Night, and The Knife, Pandora's Box, Sister Of, Miss Julie* (Arcola); *The Boy Who Climbed Out of His Face* (Shunt); *The Last Words You'll Hear* (Almeida at Latitude); *Advice for the Young at Heart* (Theatre Centre); *The Centre* (Islington Community Theatre); *The Three Sisters, The Laramie Project* (GSMD); *Snow White, US/UK Exchange,* (Old Vic New Voices); *Meat* (Bush Theatre); *Once In A Lifetime, The Eighth Continent, An Absolute Turkey* (E15); *Colors, The Criminals, House of Bones, Medea* (Drama Centre).

As Associate: *Barbershop Chronicles* (National Theatre); *Cat on a Hot Tin Roof* (Young Vic/West End); *Adler and Gibb* (Royal Court Theatre); *I'd Rather Goya Robbed Me of My Sleep Than Some Other Arsehole* (The Gate).

As Operator: *King Charles III; Chimerica; Jersusalem; Clybourne Park; Enron.*

BETHANY DUKE | Composition & Sound Designer

Beth is currently in her final year studying Theatre Sound at the Royal Central School of Speech and Drama.

Sound design and composition credits include: *The State of Things* (The Brockley Jack Theatre); *Split* (The Network Theatre); *Boots* (VAULTS 2018); *Boxman* (UK Tour); *A Fantastic Bohemian, Lovesick* (Arcola Theatre); *Little Did I Know* (Bread & Roses Theatre); *Breathe* (Tristian Bates Theatre); *Around The Block* (Etcetera Theatre); *Eros* (The White Bear Theatre).

ZOE SPURR | Lighting Designer

Zoe trained at Royal Central School of Speech and Drama.

Recent theatre includes: *The Unreturning* (Frantic Assembly / UK Tour); *Toast* (Traverse 1); *Meek* (Headlong/UK Tour); *Abigail's Party, Abi* (Queens Theatre Hornchurch/UK Tour); *Polstead* (Eastern Angles/UK Tour); *Sticky, Infinite Joy, Confidence, Natives, Collective Rage* (Southwark Playhouse); *Tiny Dynamite* (Old Red Lion); *The Phlebotomist* (Hampstead Theatre); *Not Talking* (Arcola Theatre); *Grotty* (Bunker Theatre); *Phoenix Rising, Loose Lips* (Big House Theatre Company, Site Specific); *The Beginners* (Unicorn Theatre); *Elephant* (Birmingham REP); *The Magic Flute* (Soho Theatre/UK Tour); *The Scar Test* (Soho Theatre); *Skate Hard Turn Left* (BAC); *The Drive* (UK Tour); *Hidden* (UK Tour); *Elton John's Glasses, Good Dog* (Watford Palace / UK Tour); *Erwartung / Twice Through The Heart* (for Shadwell Opera at Hackney Showroom); *The Knife of Dawn* (Camden Roundhouse); *Affection* (with Outbox Theatre, site specific at 'The Glory').

For portfolio please see zoespurrlighting.co.uk

About the Mercury Theatre

The Mercury Theatre, Colchester is the most active producing theatre in East Anglia, and is a vital centre of excellence in the East's growing creative economy. The Mercury exists to put theatre at the heart of the community it serves and to make work in Colchester that reaches audiences and generates critical attention regionally and nationally.

www.mercurytheatre.co.uk | @mercurytheatre

About Wiltshire Creative

Wiltshire Creative is a new pan-arts organisation that brings together the energy and ambition of Salisbury Arts Centre, Salisbury International Arts Festival and Salisbury Playhouse. It is an ambitious and innovative joint arts offer that secures a bright future for audiences, artists and participants. Salisbury Playhouse is part of Wiltshire Creative and is one of Britain's leading producing theatres, with a national reputation for home-grown work of the highest quality that attracts audiences from across Wiltshire, Hampshire, Dorset and beyond.

www.wiltshirecreative.co.uk | @wiltscreative

About the Unity Theatre

Unity Theatre gives audiences and participants opportunities to engage with live performances that excite, entertain and inspire. Our theatre spaces are intimate, allowing visitors to experience the exhilaration of live performance, up close. We've been behaving radically onstage since the 1930's and to this day, our theatre serves as a counterpoint to the mainstream, championing equality for diverse communities and artists.

www.unitytheatreliverpool.co.uk | @unitytheatre

To Maria Werenowska (nee Baldin), Maria Doull (nee Lusinowska) and Ryszard Bitner-Glindzicz.

To all those who passed through Siberia and Kazakhstan and to those who came after.

To telling the truth.

.

Showing through

The meteorite that doomed the dinosaur,
its ravages, are jungle-smothered now
or clouded on the teeming ocean floor.
But still from space the scarrings show.

Bombsites blossom with willow-herb and nettle,
buddleia wreathes a plot laid waste,
seaweed clings to wrecks where shellfish settle.
But still the ruins can be traced.

Close up – the painting glows, warm tones suffuse,
soften and trickle over lines,
waft round the eye, intensify, diffuse.
Stand back – and distance clarifies:

white plaster pieces roughly cut
clamp fractures that refuse to set,
patches on abrasions put
too raw to remember or forget.

Anita Debska

ACKNOWLEDGEMENT AND THANKS

This production of SILENCE has been made possible by the generous support of the following organisations:

The Mercury Theatre Colchester, Unity Theatre Liverpool, Salisbury Playhouse, Grants For The Arts, SOS Polonia, the Polish Cultural Institute, Kresy Family, Ognisko Polish Hearth Club, Lakeside Theatre, Malinka Polish Poetry Salon.

Thanks to: Daniel Buckroyd, Tracey Childs, Dan Sherer, Dilek Latif, Rhianna Howard, Jo Newman, Matthew Linley, Anita Debska, Barbara Storey, Mirka Wojnar, Arek Tylza, Jeni Draper, Christine Absalom, Anna Eliajsz, Ania Sowinski, Barbara Peirson, Thomas Edwards, Neil Jones, Tony Fisher.

Special Thanks to: Nina Finbow, Helen Bitner, a wonderful cast and creative team and everyone at the Mercury Theatre.

SILENCE (*'CICHO'*)
by Nicola Werenowska

CHARACTERS

MARIA	seventies, Polish, moved to UK as a displaced person during WW2.
EWA	fifty six, Maria's daughter, anxious and ambitious.
ANNA	twenty one, Ewa's daughter.

LANGUAGE

When characters speak in Polish, the English translation is given in brackets directly after the Polish line/s.

Action takes place in London, Reading and Warsaw between 1996 and 2016.

ACT ONE: 1996

1.1

JUNE 1996

The three women are in separate spaces.

Ewa is in her bedroom of her London house, putting on make up, drinking wine. Anna is on a train from Reading to Paddington. Maria is in her Reading bungalow, looking at old photographs.

ANNA:	8th June 1996. And I'm on a train from Reading to Paddington and I don't want to be here.
EWA:	8th June 1996. It's not a special birthday.
ANNA:	It's just Mum is so miserable on her birthday.
EWA:	50 – now that was something. Half a century!
ANNA:	Even her 50th.
EWA:	Well, some don't make it. If you look at the global picture... Poland.
ANNA:	I mean the Soviet Union was collapsing and you'd think that would be the best present ever.
EWA:	He took me to Paris. For my 50th. Well, I organised it, he was... busy, yes.
ANNA:	If I don't come back she'll act like I'm rejecting her.

EWA:	We stayed at the *Lutetia* and had *fruits de mer* and champagne at Les Ambassadors and… (*pause*) I've never been one for birthdays.
ANNA:	But if I go home, she'll nag me about the exams.
EWA:	No. When I was a child… my birthday…
ANNA:	When I was a kid, my birthdays…
EWA:	Mama… she was so much quieter than normal. So… quiet.
ANNA:	Grandad was the only one who seemed to enjoy my parties.
EWA:	And *Tatuś* (*Dad*) was just jolly. Jolly, jolly, jolly, jolly, jolly… too bloody jolly to make it real.
ANNA:	Well, Dad got me stuff, yeah.
EWA:	No parties, no friends, no English lemonade. I'm not complaining. I didn't ask. For a birthday party. I could have asked. I didn't.
ANNA:	And mum got all stressed out.
EWA:	But I was lucky. I felt lucky.
ANNA:	I know I'm lucky.
EWA:	In Poland there was civil war which the world ignored, people starving on the streets…
ANNA:	In Poland there was Marshal Law, curfews…

EWA:	And I got sweets.
ANNA:	…no sweets.

(*Pause*)

EWA:	Six, I remember turning six.
MARIA:	8 June 1946!
EWA:	All over Britain, Great Britain, with its empire and heroic Armed Forces, there are parties, fireworks, Victoria Sponge cake, and in London, the crowds are out, Londoners still skinny from rations but oozing optimism and pride, hundreds, thousands out to watch the Armed Forces strut their stuff.
MARIA:	The Brits, Great Brits!
EWA:	All corners of the globe represented, men and women from Australia, India, Africa…
MARIA:	(*Interrupts*) They forget us.
EWA:	But they forget us.
MARIA:	For Poland, tragedy.
EWA:	Victory Parade!
MARIA:	We fight. And fight. And fight. For this Stalin. (*Spits*)
EWA:	And it's my birthday!
MARIA:	Churchill, he good man. But what can he do? All world scared of Stalin.

17

EWA:	Only I'm not in Great Britain. Not on my 6th birthday.
MARIA:	Later we find out. What they are doing. These English cowards.
EWA:	I'm in Iran.
MARIA:	Jerzy, he write me letter, angry letter.
EWA:	With Mama. Me and Mama are in Iran and *Tatuś* is somewhere else.
MARIA:	From UK. He already in UK. With Army. British Army. He join in Africa. We come later.
EWA:	And I miss him.
MARIA:	But for our people – silence.
EWA:	*Tato, Tato? Gdzie jesteś? Gdzie jesteś? (Dad, Dad? Where are you? Where are you?)*
MARIA:	(*Screaming*) SILENCE!
(*Pause*)	
	8 June 1946.
EWA:	I'm in the garden at the orphanage and I'm skipping with my friends.
MARIA:	I get out of lorry at Isfahan and… hot.
EWA:	It's really hot.
MARIA:	I see her.

EWA:	I don't see Mama at first.
MARIA:	I see her many times of course. From Tehran I very often get lift. But today she... I don't know but I... all of sudden I...
EWA:	Everyone's running and shouting.
MARIA:	Running. I running.
EWA:	And then I see Mama, running towards me.
MARIA:	I push other girls to side for to get to Ewa.
EWA:	'Mama?'
MARIA:	I want to touch her, to hold her, to feel her...
EWA:	She puts her arms around me.
MARIA:	And kiss her.
EWA:	And she won't stop kissing me.
MARIA:	And kiss and kiss and kiss...
EWA:	And Mama never kisses me and it's strange and, '*Mama co robisz?*' (*Mama what are you doing?*) I ask her what she's doing.
MARIA:	*Wszystkiego najlepszego, Ewunia!* (*Happy Birthday, Ewa!*)
EWA:	She wishes me Happy Birthday and I think so maybe this is what happens when you're 6. Your mum kisses you when she never normally does.

MARIA:	I tell her we go home.
EWA:	I think we're going back to Poland.
MARIA:	She think we go back to Poland.
EWA:	*Do Polski, Mama? (To Poland, Mama?)*
MARIA:	No, no, not Poland. I tell her we go UK. Big ship.
EWA:	I'm trembling.
MARIA:	She shaking. 'You no like boat?' I asking her
EWA:	And trembling.
MARIA:	Then I remember. That journey. We crossing Caspian Sea. From Russia to Iran. Krasnovodsk to Pahlavi.
EWA:	I feel sick.
MARIA:	This boat... will be different. Will be good, I tell her.
EWA:	But I'm not listening because I want *Tatuś*!
MARIA:	I tell her to get bags and so on. 'Go now! *Proszę!' (Please!)*
EWA:	*Tatuś*!
MARIA:	When she come back with bag... this feeling... gone.
EWA:	But Dad's gone.
MARIA:	But is ok. I no want feel.

EWA:	My birthday.
MARIA:	Is no good day.
(*Pause*)	
EWA:	I wasn't what she wanted.
ANNA:	I'm just not what she wants.
EWA:	The wrong sex, the wrong day, the wrong country.
ANNA:	It's like it's never enough
EWA:	I can't blame her. The war, it did things.
ANNA:	I'm never enough.
EWA:	And I'm alright, yes. I survived.
ANNA:	Breathing down my neck and...
EWA:	We all did.
ANNA:	And I need to tell her about college (*pause*)
EWA:	And I have a good life. A beautiful daughter, talented, very talented, we're... close.
ANNA:	But I can't talk to her.
EWA:	And my husband is... hardworking,
ANNA:	And Dad won't care.
EWA:	(*Quietly*) and not openly disloyal
ANNA:	Too busy sleeping with his receptionist.

EWA: And… my parents are still alive.

ANNA: And *Dziadek* (*Grandad*) won't get it.

EWA: My breast scan was normal.

ANNA: But it's not even a big deal.

EWA: I'm lucky. (*Pause*)

ANNA: It's nothing really.

EWA: Fifty six – it's nothing these days.

ANNA: I mean like no one's died.

EWA: Nothing at all.

1.2

JUNE 1996.

Ewa's house, London. A little later that evening.

Ewa in her bedroom as in previous scene. Anna enters

ANNA:	Mum!
EWA:	Anna.
ANNA:	Are you ready?
EWA:	You're here.
ANNA:	Yeah, just about. I got stuck on a tube.
EWA:	It's lovely you've come, made the effort.
ANNA:	It's not exactly far.
EWA:	With your exams…
ANNA:	(*Interrupts*) They're almost over.

(*Pause*)

EWA:	It's still a way.
ANNA:	55 minutes from Paddington.
EWA:	If you could rely on the trains these days.
ANNA:	That's privatisation for you, when you let the Tories get…
EWA:	(*Interrupts*) Not on my birthday, Anna. (*Pause*) You'd better get yourself ready.

ANNA:	I'm fine like this. (*Beat*) It's booked for 8.
EWA:	I thought you might want to wear that purple dress. The taffeta you wore to the school…
ANNA:	We're going to be late.
EWA:	Your father's not here.
ANNA:	He's leaving work early so I'm sure he'll…
EWA:	(*Interrupts*) I appreciate the sacrifice.
ANNA:	What?
EWA:	I'm sure you'll have time to get changed.
ANNA:	I'm going like this, mum.
	(*Pause, Ewa pours glass of wine*)
EWA:	Do you want a drink?
ANNA:	No.
EWA:	You keep telling me to relax, yes?
ANNA:	Chill out a bit, yeah.
EWA:	That's what I'm doing, 'chilling out'. (*Drinks*)
(*Pause*)	
ANNA:	Mum, your new medication. Dad says…
EWA:	Does he?
ANNA:	I mean a glass is probably ok.

EWA:	Have you ever seen me drunk, Anna? (*Pause*) Have you? (*Pause*) Now have a glass! Lighten up! Your father will be here in a minute and if not, if something important has cropped up…
ANNA:	He can't help it. (*Pause*) You know, things… at the surgery…
EWA:	Absolutely! His work is very important, 'he' is very important, and let's face it, what does *Dziadek* say? 'In a war you always need doctors.' (*Pause*) Let's have another glass. It is lovely to have you back. Now tell me about the exams.
ANNA:	I could call the restaurant.
EWA:	How did they go?
ANNA:	We don't want to lose the table.
EWA:	You might get a prize again this year. You're such a….
ANNA:	(*Interrupts*) Yeah, it's harder this year.
EWA:	That's what you'd expect.
ANNA:	Yeah…
EWA:	Unless they give it to someone else.
ANNA:	What?
EWA:	The prize. In the name of fairness, the faculty could…

ANNA: (*Interrupts*) Will you stop talking about the prize. It's like not important.

EWA: (*Pause*) No, no, it's your final degree that matters.

ANNA: I can't think that far ahead. Shall I call the surgery? Just to check...

EWA: (*Interrupts*) When he's here, he's here. (*Pours more wine*)

ANNA: Mama, you'll be drunk before we get there.

EWA: I'll leave that to your father.

ANNA: He's driving.

EWA: Well, I'm pleased the exams went well.

ANNA: They... they... they didn't. Ok.

EWA: What?

ANNA: They didn't go that well.

EWA: Anna? (*Pause*) *To prawda?* (*Really?*) (*Pause*) You always underestimate yourself, *Kochanie* (*Darling*).

ANNA: I didn't finish the paper.

EWA: Well, as long as you get a 2:1 in the end.

ANNA: Yeah, I'm a long way from that.

EWA:	(*Pause*) I only got a first because I put my back into it. That's what you did then. Girls like me. 24 hours in the library.
ANNA:	My mind went blank.
EWA:	(*Pause*) Blank?
ANNA:	Yeah.
EWA:	But you answered most of the questions?
ANNA:	Some.
EWA:	What do you mean some? (*Pause*) Eighty per cent? (*Pause*) Fifty per cent? (*Pause*) Anna? (*Pause*) Did you answer anything?
ANNA:	I tried.
EWA:	Anna, this is your degree, it's… (*Phone rings*)
ANNA:	Shit!
EWA:	Anna!
ANNA:	Yeah, it's probably the restaurant wondering if we're…
EWA:	(*Interrupts*) It's probably your father. You answer it, please.
ANNA:	Ok. (*Picks up phone*) Hello? (*Pause*) *Babcia*? (*Pause*) What? (*Pause*) *Dziadek*, what…? (*Pause*) Hospital? Hang on, hang on *Babcia*. (*To Ewa*) She's talking Polish, I can't…

EWA:	(*Picking up phone*) Mama? (*Pause*) *Co?* (*What?*) (*Pause*) *Szpital?* (*Hospital?*) (*Pause*) Is he ok? (*Pause*) *Ale jest ok?*(*But he is ok?*) Is he ok, Mama? *Tatuś?* (*Pause*) *Jak to, nie wiesz?* (*What do you mean you don't know?*) What do you mean? (*Pause*) Ok, I'm coming now.
ANNA:	*Dziadek…?*
EWA:	He's collapsed, apparently.
ANNA:	Is he…?
EWA:	A&E, Barks hospital.
ANNA:	Is he ok, mum?
EWA:	I've… got to go to A&E. I've got to go now.
ANNA:	Yeah. Shall I drive you?
EWA:	You…?
ANNA:	Dad's put me on the license.
EWA:	No.
ANNA:	So how…
EWA:	(*Interrupts*) Your father's not here, Anna. Your father is never here when I need him.
ANNA:	It's not Dad's…
EWA:	Your father is fucking somewhere someone else.

ANNA:	What...?
EWA:	Somewhere else. Not here.
ANNA:	That's not what...
EWA:	I'll get a cab.
ANNA:	It's a long way.
EWA:	I don't care.
ANNA:	I'll come with you.
EWA:	No.
ANNA:	Mama!
EWA:	Wait for Dad and...
ANNA:	Please!
EWA:	Come later. *Dziadek* may be home soon. It could all be a false alarm. I'll phone you when I know what's happening.
ANNA:	Are you sure you're...?
EWA:	Mascara.
ANNA:	You look great, Mama.
EWA:	(*Pause*) Do I...?
ANNA:	Forget about the mascara.
EWA:	Yes.

(*Pause. They look at one another. Ewa exits.*)

1.3

JUNE 1996.

Barks Hospital, Reading. Later that evening.

Ewa is finishing a conversation on a payphone, Maria is at a distance, self absorbed, suddenly notices Ewa.

MARIA:	*Ewunia.*
EWA:	Mama, are you ok?
MARIA:	*Gdzie poszłaś? (Where did you go?)*
EWA:	To phone Patrick. I told you
MARIA:	*Kogo? (Who?)*
EWA:	Patrick. My husband. *(Quietly)* If you could call him that.
MARIA:	*Co? (What?)*
EWA:	He didn't offer to come. I would have said no of course.
MARIA:	*Ewunia?*
EWA:	He didn't offer. *(Pause)* Do you want a cup of tea, Mama?
MARIA:	*Herbatę? (Tea?)*
EWA:	Yes, there's a cafeteria upstairs.
MARIA:	*Twój Tata. (Your Dad.)*

EWA: Dad's resting now. We have to wait for the consultant, yes?

MARIA: *Co?* (*What?*)

EWA: *Na lekarza, Mama.* (*For the doctor, Mama.*)

MARIA: *Aha.* (*pause*) He want funeral in Poland.

EWA: Funeral?

MARIA: *W Polce.* (*In Poland.*)

EWA: Mama, he's not... *Jest ok.* (*He's ok.*) Why are you talking about a funeral?

MARIA: *Warszawa, Świętego Krzyża.*

EWA: Yes, I know the church. I've been there, after the wall, remember? Me and *Tatuś?* What he'd always wanted, to go back. Do you remember?

MARIA: *Oczywiście.* (*Of course.*)

EWA: (*Pause*)... he's going to be fine. (*Pause*) You heard what the doctor said. (*Pause*) Mama, did you understand what the doctor said?

MARIA: *Chyba tak.* (*Maybe*)

EWA: A chance. *Szansa.* (*a chance*) He said there's a chance.

MARIA: (*Indicating*) *Mała szansa.* (*A small chance*)

EWA: Well, they have to say that. If they promise you a complete recovery and then... you could take them to court.

MARIA: *Do sądu? (To court?)*

EWA: Happens all the time in America.

MARIA: *No tak. (yeah)*

EWA: We have to be positive. Patrick said they can do wonderful things these days. He says *Tatuś* is going to be absolutely fine.

MARIA: *Dla mnie, to już nieważne. (For me, it's not important)*

EWA: What's not important?

MARIA: *Ale dla niego tak. (For him, it's very important.)*

EWA: What...?

MARIA: *Pogrzeb w Polsce (The funeral in Poland)*

EWA: Stop talking about a..., Mama. Please. Stop it! I know where *Tatuś* wants to be buried, ok, but... this... this is not the right moment. He's alive, yes?

MARIA: *Ewunia.*

EWA: There is a pulse, there is a beating heart, there is a person. He is not dead.

MARIA: *Cicho! (Be quiet!)*

EWA: Stop talking about him like he's dead. Stop it!

MARIA:	*Cicho!* (*Be quiet!*)
EWA:	He's alive and you're... you're a pessimist.
MARIA:	*Jestem realistkq.* (*I'm a realist.*)
EWA:	That's not being realistic. That's... that's... Jesus!
MARIA:	*Ewunia.*

(*Anna enters, runs up to Ewa & Maria.*)

ANNA:	Mama. *Babcia.*
EWA:	Anna.
ANNA:	Where's *Dziadek?*
EWA:	What are you...?
MARIA:	*Malutka.* (*Little one.*)
EWA:	Darling, you're supposed to be at home with...
ANNA:	I want to see *Dziadek.*
EWA:	With your father...?
ANNA:	He's got held up.
EWA:	Did you call the restaurant?
ANNA:	No.
EWA:	Oh. Well, I think we....
ANNA:	Fuck the restaurant, Mama!

EWA: Anna!

ANNA: Can I see him now, please?

EWA: He's asleep, darling. We're not allowed in right now. It was a big heart attack and...

ANNA: Oh my God!

EWA: He's going to be fine.

ANNA: Is he?

EWA: Absolutely.

MARIA: *Zobaczymy.* (*We will see.*)

ANNA: What?

EWA: Yes, he'll be fine once...

ANNA: She didn't say that. (*To Maria*) *Babcia?* (*Granny?*)

EWA: I'm going to make that phone call. The restaurant. I don't like letting people down. They could use the table for someone else.

(*Moves to phone*)

MARIA: *Ona nie chce słyszeć prawdy.* (*She doesn't want to hear the truth.*)

ANNA: What's true?

(*Beat*)

      Babcia?

34

MARIA: *Nic.*

(*Beat*)

              Bardzo cię kocha. (*He loves you very much.*)

ANNA: I love him too.

MARIA: *No tak.* (*Yeah.*)

(*Maria and Anna look at one another. Ewa finishes call.*)

1.4

JUNE 1996.

Warsaw Church, funeral service. A few weeks later.

Three women sitting next to each other in church.

EWA: And at the funeral in the *Bazylika Świętego Krzyża*, she thinks of Stalin.

ANNA: She's wishing she could understand what's being said but she can't.

MARIA: She think nothing.

EWA: Not the butchery, the murders, the mass murders, the raping and looting, the camps, the civil war, the betrayal of all betrayals in the Warsaw Uprising, the destruction of the city in which she's now standing. (*Pause*) She thinks of Stalin's death.

ANNA: She can't make sense of it. But that's cool. They're all the same. Funerals. She imagines they're all the same. She hasn't been to one before. But you say nice things about the person, you have to. She's thinking *Dziadek* is the past now, will always be the past unless you can be present when you're dead but you can't.

MARIA: She no want be here. She no want remember.

EWA: She remembers.

ANNA: She remembers.

MARIA: When he die, he look at her. She think when last time he look at her? Like this. When he stop looking?

EWA: The fifth of March 1953. She's twelve years old and racing home from school, tiptoeing into the house because *Tatuś* is on nightshift and… there he is. *Tatuś*, not asleep, awake, and with… a beer in his hand. And she thinks she's done something bad but he's smiling. Like really smiling with his face and his eyes and he picks her up and he doesn't pick her up anymore. He's swinging her around and now she thinks she must have passed the 11+ after all. It must have been a mistake that's taken them a year to find out. He is that happy holding her. *Tatuś* what is it? *'On jest martwy,' (He's dead)*, he says. 'He dead.'

ANNA: 1983. She's seven and there's a Polish pope and *Dziadek's* laughing so hard he's crying but he's not sad. And she feels happy too and she hasn't even met the Pope but he looks nice, a bit old but nice. *Dziadek* says a Polish pope could change the world and there could be an end to the Iron Curtain. But *Babcia* says a pope can change nothing. And Mama says, 'We'll see', because that's what she says a lot.

MARIA: 1939. Her wedding. Here. This church. *No tak. (Yeah.)* August. Before bombing and fire and Nazis. *(Pause)* And Russians. *(Pause)* He

37

look at her. And day is beautiful, sun and no cloud and hot. In church maybe 300 people. But he look at her. Her only. And in his face, she see... no fear. And she think she lucky, she think he will... protect me. She excited. Very. Honeymoon – will be here in *Warszawa*, and after will be move to Lwów. Lwów! He have job, at university, for research. (*Pause*) She think, now I safe.

EWA: *Tatuś* who's dead? Who is it? Who's dead? 'Józef Stalin,' he says and he's smiling again. '*Teraz mamy nadzieję.*' (*Now we have hope*) 'Now we have hope.' '*Możemy wrócić.*' (*We can go back*), he says. 'We can go back.' But she's panicking. Back to Poland! What he wants more than anything, but there are soldiers there with guns and she can't do Polish grammar and where will they live and you can't even get sweets there and... '*Cicho!*' (*silence!*), he says. 'Silence.' '*Pewnego dnia* (*One day*), one day, *Malutka*.' She doesn't ask when.

ANNA: She understands nothing. It's like a bad dream. She feels... Why the fuck did she stop learning Polish? Why the fuck did Mama let her? Bring on the bloody vodka, she thinks! No, no, that's too stereotypical, too old Poland, too Daily Mail. It's changing here. She can feel it. She remembers five years ago. Everything was so dark... it's like the city's waking up. (*Pause*) She wants to wake up too.

(*Pause*) To what she wants and to what she doesn't. She wonders could I live here? This city? Could I belong? In Warsaw?

MARIA: But no one safe. You can forget but you can't make disappear. After eating, drinking, dancing, she see it. Fear. Everywhere, every face. They will come now, the Germans. Not if but when. And every day now from Germany they coming, Jews and others, they want escape. (*Pause*) War. She say it on tongue. She no know what it mean.

EWA: The things you never ask... She thinks how often he said he loved her and did she say it enough back? And was she really a disappointment in the end? She thinks she'll live differently now. Better. A better daughter. A better mother.

ANNA: If he was alive, she'd ask his advice. 'I can't go back there *Dziadek*!' 'But why not, *Malutka*?' 'Because I... I... I can't... I'm not in the right space to study, and not psychology, it's all maths and... and I want to go to Poland.' 'To Poland? Good idea, why not?' (*Pause*) Would he say that? Would he?

MARIA: When he stop looking? Her husband. When...? (*Pause*)When...? When she stop? (*Suddenly shouting*) *Jerzy!*

EWA: When they lower the coffin, the tears come.

ANNA: She cries through the service.

MARIA: She no cry.

EWA: But he's back, she thinks. Silent and dead and home.

ANNA: Could this be her home?

MARIA: Nothing.

1.5

JUNE 1996.

On a plane to Heathrow, the following day.

Maria sitting in the middle of a row of 3. The other two women are asleep. Voice control message: 'PLEASE TAKE YOUR SEATS. FLIGHT LO702 Warsaw Frederic Chopin to London Heathrow.'

Maria closes her eyes as if asleep. Opens them, looks around.

MEMORY

MARIA: June 1940. Lwów. (*pause*) He come to her that night. She in nursery. Ewa, she waking very often for milk and she go sleep in chair. Is first time after baby come and she think maybe will be some pain, but she want. This man. She look at him. He kiss her. 'I want forget,' he say. 'Me also,' she say. (*Pause*) For him, very hard. Now is no work, but every day he leaving house at seven like always, she no know what he do and when and who and…she no ask. To know nothing – is better. (*Pause, smiling*) There is no pain. And for moment – he back. The man she love. The life she want. (*Pause*) For her is hard also, but in nursery with Ewa, she happy. She pretend – there are no Russians, no shootings at night, no knocking on door, no friends disappear. (*Pause*) When is over, he look at her. 'Now is time,' he say. 'They coming.'

41

'When?'

'Soon.'

'But how you know this?'

'Get ready!' he says. 'Do it!' And he shouting and Ewa she crying. He slam door and she pick up Ewa, (*Soothing baby, rocking and humming lullaby*) Soon Ewa she sleep again but she no want stop. (*Continues humming, rocking*) She make promise, to Ewa. 'I keep you alive, *Malutka*!' After, she no sleep. When knock come at 3 in morning, she waiting. She ready.

1.6

JULY 1996.

Maria's flat, Reading. A few weeks later.

Maria in armchair. Anna and Ewa sorting papers in separate but adjoining space. Ewa gives up, moves to Mama, offers her the rest of a barely touched piece of cake.

EWA: Do you want some cake?

MARIA: *Nie. (No.)*

EWA: Are you sure?

MARIA: *Tak. (Yes.)*

EWA: Mama, you must eat. *Musisz jeść. (You must eat.)*

MARIA: *(To self) Dlaczego? (Why?)*

EWA: Everyone has to eat, Mama, you'll waste away. *(Pause)* Anna's still sorting through it all. *(Pause)* there's a mountain of papers in *Tatuś's* bureau. *(Pause)* The amount of stuff he kept. You open a drawer and out it flows – his life spilling out higgedly piggedly – photos and bills, receipts, newspaper cuttings... why do you keep one thing and not another?

MARIA: *Cicho! (Be quiet!)*

EWA: Mama...?

MARIA: *Cicho!(Be quiet!)*

43

EWA:	Don't tell me to be quiet, Mama. (*Pause*) It's what I'm here for. To talk to you. You know, conversation. If Anna and myself didn't drop by, you... You don't talk to anyone Mama, you don't go out, you don't do anything.
MARIA:	*On nie żyje.* (*He's dead.*)
EWA:	Yes he's dead but you're here. You're alive and you... you have to carry on, yes. We all do. (*Maria shrugs, pause*) She's doing a good job over there.
MARIA:	*Co?* (*What?*)
EWA:	Anna. She's very organised. Well, it's given her something to do and she's got the time. It's at least two months before she goes back.
MARIA:	*Gdzie?* (*Where?*)
EWA:	To university. (*pause*) She has her summer job as well of course. That keeps her busy and she seems to like working in Marks.
MARIA:	Spencer?
EWA:	Yes, in Marks. Just to gain some experience. And she's saving up for when she goes back. They've cut maintenance grants now, did you know about that, Mama? Anna's lucky, of course. With Patrick's salary, there won't be a problem for her obviously. Mama, are you listening?

(*Anna enters*)

44

ANNA: I'm done!

EWA: All finished?

ANNA: I wish. There's stuff... I don't know what to bin and what not to.

EWA: Just do what you think best, darling.

ANNA: Yeah, but some of the older stuff. It's all in Polish and...

EWA: We'll ask Mama if you think it's important.

ANNA: Stuff like this. (*Handing Ewa an official looking document*) Mama? (*Pause*) What is it?

EWA: (*Reading*) *Akt urodzenia?* (*A birth certificate?*) It's a birth certificate.

ANNA: Really?

EWA: March 17, 1941. Siberia.

ANNA: What?

EWA: *Mama* and *Tatuś*, they were in Siberia, in 1941.

ANNA: And...?

EWA: (*To Maria*) Mama. Mamo, *co to jest?* (*What's this?*) (*Handing her document*) (*Pause*)

MARIA: *Nie wiem.* (*I don't know*)

EWA: You don't know?

MARIA: *Nie.* (*No.*)

EWA: You must know.

MARIA: *Jestem zmęczona. (I'm tired.)*

EWA: You're tired.

MARIA: *Mogę prosić kawę?(I'd like some coffee, please.)*

EWA: Coffee, yes, good idea. We'll make some coffee. Anna, would you...?

ANNA: Ok.

EWA: *(To Maria) Co to jest? (What is it?)*

MARIA: *Nie wiem.(I don't know.)*

EWA: Mama, of course you know. You must know. *Musisz wiedzieć. (You must know) (Pause)* Ok, ok, let me tell you.

ANNA: Mama!

EWA: Make the coffee!

ANNA: It's just you're...

EWA: *Akt urodzenia. (A birth certificate)* It's a birth certificate, Mama.

MARIA: *No tak. (Right)*

EWA: And your name is on it. Yes. Can you see that? Do you need your glasses? Look, you are registered as the parent of a child, as its mother, and *Tatuś* is registered as its father.

MARIA: *Nie pamiętam. (I can't remember.)*

46

EWA:	You can't remember!
ANNA:	Calm down, Mama.
EWA:	(*To Anna*) *Cicho!* (*Be quiet!*) This is important. (*To Maria*) *Mamo?*
MARIA:	*Nie przypominam sobie tego aktu urodzenia.* (*I can't remember the certificate.*)
EWA:	Who is it? *Kto to jest?* (*Who is it?*) Who the hell is it?
ANNA:	Mum!
EWA:	*Cicho!* (*Be quiet!*)
ANNA:	You're scaring her.
EWA:	This... this is scaring me.
ANNA:	Don't scare her!
EWA:	(*To Maria*) Tell me. Tell me. Mama. Tell me. Mama.
MARIA:	*Chłopiec.* (*A boy.*)
EWA:	*Tak.* (*yes.*)
MARIA:	*Wiktor.*
EWA:	(*Reading*) *Wiktor Jerzy Kowalski.*
MARIA:	*No tak.* (*Yeah.*)
EWA:	You... you and *Tatuś*...
MARIA:	*Nie pamiętam.* (*I can't remember.*)

EWA: You can't remember the child. This child. Wiktor.

MARIA: *Nie widzę jego twarzy. (I can't see his face.)*

ANNA: What's she saying?

EWA: She can't remember his face.

ANNA: Is she the mother?

EWA: It's her name for god's sake. *To jest Twoje dziecko, Mama. Tak? (This is your child, Mama? Yes?)* Your child?

MARIA: *Mój syn. (My son.)*

EWA: Her son.

ANNA: So, your... brother...?

EWA: I don't have a brother.

ANNA: But if *Babcia* had a baby...

EWA: *(Interrupts)* No, no, no, no, no! No!

ANNA: Please Mama, calm down.

EWA: What happened? *Muszę wiedzieć, co się stało. (I need to know what happened.)*

ANNA: Give her a chance!

EWA: *Mamo, Powiedz mi, co się stało. Powiedz mi! (Tell me what happened, Mama. Tell me!)*

ANNA: Mum!

EWA:	Stay out of this! (*To Maria*) Tell me!
MARIA:	In Siberia come also babies.
EWA:	*Gdzie on jest? Gdzie jest Wiktor?* (*Where is he? Where's Wiktor?*)
MARIA:	But they die. Most often die.
EWA:	No.
MARIA:	My baby, Wiktor, he die.
EWA:	No!
MARIA:	In camp, too cold, no food. You can no live with baby. To die, is better.
EWA:	I didn't die.
MARIA:	*Byłaś większa.* (*You were bigger.*)
EWA:	What... seven weeks old when the Russians came calling? Two when the camp was liberated?
MARIA:	*I silniejsza.* (*And stronger.*)
EWA:	Stronger!
MARIA:	For you, I have milk. For Wiktor, no.
EWA:	I can't... I can't remember. I can't remember my brother.
MARIA:	*Tak jest lepiej.* (*It's better.*)
EWA:	How is it better? To pretend something didn't happen. I had a brother and you didn't tell

	me. Jesus! Mama! (*beat*) When it happened. You must have told me something when it happened. One day there's a baby and the next day there's not. Didn't I notice?
MARIA:	*Oczywiście. że tak.* (*Yes, of course.*) But there. That place. People they all time dying.
EWA:	What did you tell me about my brother?
MARIA:	*Powiedzieliśmy ci, że poszedł do nieba.* (*We told you he'd gone to heaven.*)
EWA:	Heaven!
MARIA:	*Właśnie.* (*Yeah.*)
(*Pause*)	
EWA:	You let me forget him. You buried all memory of him.
MARIA:	*We wanted to move on.*
EWA:	Move on! Well that's a joke because you've moved nowhere.
ANNA:	Mama!
EWA:	All these years and what do you do? Sit there like a snow queen, frozen solid to that bloody chair. Don't you think I had a right to know?
ANNA:	Stop it!
MARIA:	(*To Ewa*) *Nie.* (*No.*)
EWA:	No!? Jesus!

MARIA:	We make decision.
EWA:	You stupid woman. (*Shaking Maria*) You stupid, stupid, stupid, stupid woman.
ANNA:	Stop it, Mum.
EWA:	What sort of a mother are you? Answer me!
ANNA:	Leave her alone.
EWA:	*Odpowiedz mi!* (*Answer me!*)
ANNA:	*Mama*, please, you're...
EWA:	Shut up!
ANNA:	STOP! (*Physically pulls Ewa away from Maria. pause*)
EWA:	My God. What...what was I doing... Mama...?
ANNA:	You... you disgust me.
ANNA:	*Babcia*, are you ok?
MARIA:	*Jestem ok.* (*I'm ok.*)
ANNA:	*Babcia.* (*She takes Maria's hands, comforts her, cautiously touches her on face. There is an awkward warmth.*)
EWA:	(*To Anna*) Do you know what it was like? For me? Growing up here?
ANNA:	What do you think it was like for her in Siberia?

EWA: I was there too, yes.

ANNA: Yeah, but you were two years old, you can't remember.

EWA: So that makes it alright?

ANNA: That's not what I...

EWA: (*interrupts*) Here. In Reading. After... I lived their pain, Anna. What happened to them. Every day I lived it.

ANNA: Yeah and so do I.

EWA: What?

ANNA: You. The way you are...

EWA: No.

ANNA: (*Shrugs. Pause.*) I'm not going back to uni.

EWA: What?

ANNA: I hate the course. I failed the exams.

EWA: You didn't fail, you... Anna, this is... ridiculous. You can't abandon your degree.

ANNA: What, are you ashamed of me?

EWA: No, no. Not ashamed. No. I... I... what will I tell people?

ANNA: What people? You don't have to worry about *Dziadek* now.

MARIA:	*Zawsze robi to, co chce. (She always does what he wants.)*
EWA:	No, no. I married Patrick didn't I? *Tatuś* certainly didn't want that.
MARIA:	*On miał rację. (He was right.)*
EWA:	Yes. Maybe. Maybe he was right.
ANNA:	Why don't you leave him?
EWA:	What?
ANNA:	Dad.
EWA:	Anna…
ANNA:	I know about…
EWA:	Stop! Stop this!
ANNA:	I'm not a kid anymore.
EWA:	It's really none of your business.
ANNA:	It's not like Dad makes you happy.
EWA:	No one makes anyone happy, Anna.
ANNA:	Yes they do.
EWA:	Well you're young and that's what young people think. (*Pause*) With you… I… I wanted it to be different, Anna. For you. I wanted to be different.
ANNA:	(*Pause*) I'm going to Poland.

EWA: What?

ANNA: Because I want to.

MARIA: *Prose kawę? (Coffee, please.)*

ANNA: *Babcia?*

MARIA: *Dobrze (It's ok.)*

EWA: Poland!

MARIA: *Dlaczego nie? Why not?*

EWA: Why not? Why...? (*Anna and Maria embrace,
            hold each other, this time without awkwardness.
            Ewa watches to one side, alone. Whispering to
            self*) Wiktor! Wiktor!

1.7

AUGUST 1996 / APRIL 1942

Anna is on a plane to Warsaw. Maria is on a boat crossing the Caspian sea to Pahlavi.

MARIA: April 1942, Krasnovodsk to Pahlavi.

ANNA: August 1996, London Heathrow to Warsaw Okencie.

(*Pause*)

ANNA: On the plane she can't breathe.

MARIA: On boat she dying.

ANNA: *Dziadek* is dead.

MARIA: Everyone dying.

ANNA: She can't think.

MARIA: They think this. She think this.

ANNA: She thinks the plane will crash over the English Channel.

MARIA: She think she die in Caspian sea.

ANNA: She's flown loads before.

MARIA: Many dead before of course, *oczywiście*, (*Of course*), but boat is...

ANNA: Fuck!

MARIA: *O Boże!* (*Oh my God!*)

(*Pause. Both women struggle to breathe*)

ANNA: The plane's full.

MARIA: Is crowded and they no find seat.

ANNA: Every seat taken.

MARIA: Everyone standing.

ANNA: And she can't...

MARIA: Stand and fall,

ANNA: Spinning!

MARIA: Stand and fall.

ANNA: There's no one to help her.

MARIA: Jerszy, he hold Ewa, he no help her.

ANNA: No one.

MARIA: No one help her.

TOGETHER: No one.

(*Retches*)

ANNA: She feels sick.

MARIA: Everyone sick.

ANNA: It's not the turbulence.

MARIA: Before boat they eating fish from Polish Army for to help them but fish bad and they ill, everyone.

ANNA: Her stomach cramping.

MARIA: (*Clutching her stomach*) *Jej brzuch!* (*Her belly!*)

ANNA: Help!

MARIA: *Pomóżcie mi!* (*Help me.*)

(*Pause*)

ANNA: She thinks this is it.

MARIA: She dying.

ANNA: She's too scared to go to the toilet.

MARIA: People push very quickly for to get to toilet and Jerzy, he standing all time.

ANNA: She can't stand up.

MARIA: All time, Ewa, she in his arms, 24 hour, 36 hour.

ANNA: The journey lasts forever.

MARIA: Long time, but he hold her.

ANNA: Fucking ever!

MARIA: He no sing.

ANNA: Why is she here?

(*Pause*)

MARIA: When they get off boat at Pahlavi, Jerzy, he fall to ground.

ANNA:	When she gets off the plane at Warsaw airport, she's... ok.
MARIA:	She think he faint but, no, he kiss ground.
ANNA:	Like really ok.
MARIA:	*'Dziękuję!'* (*Thank* you) he say.
ANNA:	(*Whispers*) 'Thank you.'
MARIA:	But now she falling also but she no help this.
ANNA:	She's steady on her feet again.
MARIA:	She no breathe (*Trying to breathe*)
ANNA:	It's like... she feels...
MARIA:	...and... falling... and... black.
ANNA:	She feels light again.
MARIA:	All black.
ANNA:	Warsaw!
MARIA:	Warszawa!

ACT TWO: 1996 – 2006

2.1

AUTUMN 1996.

The women are in different spaces. Anna is in Warsaw. Ewa in her London house and Maria in her bungalow in Reading.

ANNA: And in Warsaw she breathes.

EWA: She can't breathe.

MARIA: My granddaughter!

ANNA: She breathes and walks and weeps and weeps and walks and breathes and walks some more, losing herself to the city's pasts, remembering the stories *Dziadek* told her, inventing those he didn't, imagining the life he lived here, and the life he could have lived if…, imagining until the boundaries blur and she no longer knows what's true and what's not.

EWA: Her brother.

MARIA: My Anna!

ANNA: And one evening in the old town, as dusk descends on the *Stary Rynek*, with a beer in her hand, she stares in amazement at the fake authenticity of the buildings, the bravery of the survivors, reconstructing hope from rubble… and then in her mouth (*Spitting*) disgust! The bloody Allies. Scared to stand up to Stalin. Fuck those British cowards! (*Pause*)

And suddenly... the British... Britishness, it's... it's outside of her somehow, weird, but somehow and she... she is... she breathes.

EWA: (*Trying to breathe*) This sensation.

MARIA: Another person. To feel again.

ANNA: She leaves her beer, and she's walking again, walking and walking, past the Hotel Bristol, down the Royal route, past the university, did *Dziadek* study here? She doesn't want to stand out, not here of all places, but she does. This is 1996 and the city's still downtrodden from Soviet oppression. And it's not just her clothes and hairstyle that mark her out - the way she walks, the confidence she embodies contrasting with the sadness of the faces she sees, expressions that want to believe in a future but hold... distrust. (*Pause*) She continues walking.

EWA: She wants to go out.

MARIA: She think of Anna. Many times.

ANNA: She doesn't stop, can't, won't...

EWA: She can't.

MARIA: And of him. How he want love her. How she cold. How he no angry. Sad maybe, yes, but every day smiling, every day joke or some such.

ANNA:	She wants to walk herself into the fabric of the city, crossing the bridge to Praga, moving beyond the outskirts, climbing *Pałac Kultury i Nauki*, thinking it wasn't even there… and how would *Dziadek* and *Babcia* have imagined it all?
EWA:	No photos.
MARIA:	She think, will he forgive her?
ANNA:	Some time passes and some more.
EWA:	There are no photos.
MARIA:	She think, will she forgive him?
ANNA:	And then one day she stops weeping.
EWA:	(*Crying*)
ANNA:	She finds herself outside a newsagent, goes inside and there are postcards.
EWA:	She sees him.
MARIA:	One day she get postcard from Anna.
ANNA:	The tomb of the unknown soldier.
EWA:	There are no photos, but she sees him
ANNA/MARIA:	(*Reading*) 'Dear *Babcia*…'
EWA:	And in her dreams.
ANNA:	She signs off, 'I love you.' '*Kocham Cię.*' (*I love you.*)

MARIA: *Kochanie! (Darling!)*

EWA: She cries all day.

ANNA: She breathes.

MARIA: *Kochana! (Darling!)*

EWA: She can't breathe. (*Pause*)

MARIA: She open windows in bungalow and she clean.

ANNA: She gets a job. The tears dry up and she can see a different city...

EWA: She's always seen him, always known. Somewhere.

MARIA: On her knees with broom and mop and water and everything. She breathe.

ANNA: ...not one shrouded by the colours of a past,

EWA: Always, always, always.

ANNA: but a city waking up to the daylight, to possibility and... She's teaching English. She's been here a month, it's time. She teaches English and learns Polish. She has twenty students, all keen, all excited.

MARIA: One day she find box.

EWA: She tells... she tries to tell Patrick how she used to pretend. That she had a brother. Other children had imaginary friends, why

not? It was harmless. She was an only child.
Lonely.

ANNA: Mareczek is different from the rest.

MARIA: And inside shoes. For baby.

EWA: Patrick thinks she's lost it.

ANNA: Equally keen but quiet, no, studious, he asks
                 for extra lessons, one on one. He doesn't put
                 it like that he doesn't know the phrase. 'By
                 ourself' he says,

MARIA: Not real shoes. For to keep warm.

EWA: 'You've never mentioned a brother before,' he
                 says.

ANNA: and already in that phrase she thinks
                 somehow she is part of him and he part of her
                 and...

MARIA: Before shoes are belonging to another baby.
                 A dead baby. Jerzy, he take. He say 'I sorry'
                 to father of dead baby, but he take, and she
                 no think her child will die also.

EWA: Patrick!

ANNA: and she thinks of the boys she dated at uni
                 and that they meant nothing.

MARIA: She happy. In Siberia. Not all time, no, no, is
                 hunger always and Ewa she look thin, very,
                 like stick, but she playing, smiling, and soon
                 will be new baby.

EWA:	They don't mention divorce.
ANNA:	They meet in the *Nowy Świat* café on the Royal Route. He asks her why she's in Warsaw. She explains she's half Polish and he laughs. He's in property, he says. Buying old flats and renovating them. Property, he explains, is big business in Warsaw. Buy now and in ten years. Now she's laughing. A property boom in Warsaw that's... unthinkable. Stop it!
EWA:	'Stop talking about Wiktor,' he says.
ANNA:	They're laughing together.
MARIA:	Labour long and hard and she sick and tear and scream...
EWA:	He ups her pills.
MARIA:	But he cry, he no blue, he cry and poo and suck. And she have milk!
ANNA:	Later, some weeks later, in bed in his flat in the *Nowe Miasto*, he asks her about her family and why she doesn't talk about them much apart from her grandparents. She hasn't got an answer.
EWA:	It's not the answer.
MARIA:	Milk not enough. And is also Ewa. And...
ANNA:	'For Polish people, family very important,' he says.

EWA:	And Wiktor is everywhere. She sees him everywhere – as a boy, a teenager, a young man off to study at the academy. Sometimes she imagines him going to war which is ridiculous because if he'd have lived he'd have come here to the UK with her. To safety.
MARIA:	And he's gone.
ANNA:	He says one day he will take her to Kielce and she can't teach English in Warsaw forever. Why not? She asks. He says you have to think of the future.
EWA:	There is no future.
MARIA:	After…
ANNA:	But for her there is only the present.
EWA:	Only the past.
MARIA:	She selfish.
ANNA:	And he, Mareczek is the present.
EWA:	Nothing else.
MARIA:	Selfish woman!
ANNA:	Months are passing.
EWA:	Sometimes she thinks about Anna.
MARIA:	She keep shoes.
ANNA:	Christmas is coming and she doesn't mind the cold.

EWA:	She doesn't know what to buy her.
ANNA:	Mareczek gets the train from Warsaw to Kielce.
MARIA:	She no give to next baby.
EWA:	For Christmas.
ANNA:	'You can't stay in the city on your own,' he says. 'You have to go home.'
MARIA:	Next soon be dead baby.
ANNA:	But she's happy here. In his flat in *Aleje Jerozolimskie*.
EWA:	Has she lost her?
MARIA:	She no want be selfish.
ANNA:	She can breathe here.
EWA:	(*Hyperventilates*)
MARIA:	She breathe.

2.2

CHRISTMAS EVE, 1996.

Ewa in her London house preparing the table for Wigilia. Anna has arrived and Maria is on her way in a taxi.

EWA:	*Wigilia.* (*Christmas Eve*)
ANNA:	She can't miss Christmas Eve.
MARIA:	(*Excited*) *Wigilia.* (*Christmas Eve*)
ANNA:	She helps Mama to set the table.
EWA:	She sets the table…
ANNA:	And tries to stop thinking about how expensive her ticket was.
EWA:	…with empty places for Wiktor and *Dziadek*.
ANNA:	Mama serves *Barszcz* and talks non-stop about Wiktor.
EWA:	She knows he won't come.
MARIA:	She coming! Anna!
ANNA:	But nothing about *Dziadek*. It's as if he never existed.
MARIA:	She very excited.
ANNA:	And she feels…
MARIA:	And sad, of course.

ANNA: She feels that for Mama she doesn't exist either.

EWA: She imagines him – Wiktor. Walking into the room.

ANNA: And Dad's not even here.

EWA: He'd be 54, Wiktor. If he...middle aged, like her.

ANNA: And where's *Babciu*? (*To Ewa*) 'Mama, shouldn't *Babcia* be...?'

MARIA: (*as if entering house and seeing Anna*) *Malutka!* (*Little one!*)

ANNA: (*running to Maria and hugging her*) *Wesołych Świąt, Babciu!* (*Happy Christmas, Babcia!*)

MARIA: *Wesołych Świąt, Kochana!* (*Happy Christmas, darling!*)

EWA: (*Laughing hysterically*) Middle aged!!

MARIA: Ewa! (*Kisses Ewa politely*)

EWA: *Mama, proszę, Usiądź!* (*Mama, please, sit down!*)

MARIA: I sit next to Anna.

EWA: Wiktor, that's... no...

ANNA: Mama?

EWA: No. (*Tries to gain control of herself, turning away from others*)

68

ANNA: *Babcia* is so happy to see her

MARIA: *Kochana!*

ANNA: And she won't stop asking about Warsaw.

MARIA: *Jaką macie tam pogodę? (What's the weather like?)*

ANNA: 'Yeah lots of snow.' (*Beat*) But Mama says nothing and doesn't touch her salmon.

EWA: She thinks about dying.

MARIA: She think first Christmas hard. Very hard. Jerzy – he gone.

ANNA: She asks Mama if she'll visit her in Warsaw.

EWA: That people don't stop dying because it's Christmas Eve.

MARIA: But she survive. *No tak. (Yes.)* She here.

ANNA: She asks again.

MARIA: And she lucky. Now she have Anna. (*To Anna*) 'And you come again here, *Malutka!* Soon. For to visit.'

ANNA: Of course I'll be back, *Babciu*. I promise.

EWA: She promises to visit Anna in the New Year.

MARIA: In New Year.

EWA: But how will she ever leave the house.

ANNA:	She loves seeing Babcia... She wants to go back.
EWA:	She wants to die.
MARIA:	She alive.
ANNA:	To living.
EWA:	She wishes he'd survived instead of her.
ANNA:	To Warsaw.
MARIA:	Warszawa.
EWA:	He'd be alive and she'd be dead.
ANNA:	If Mama had died and Wiktor was alive, she wouldn't be here.

2.3

2000

The women are in Warsaw, Reading and London as in start Scene 2.1.

ANNA: Back in Warsaw, she throws herself at the city and tries not to notice that Mama doesn't visit. She asks her again and again and again and then she stops asking. There's her work and there's Mareczek, and the weeks turn to months and years and suddenly a new millennium is approaching. The 21st century: she's a fluent Polish speaker now, and Mareczek owns 20 properties and then 100 and... and the sky's the limit! They eat out at the Jazz Café and the Hotel Bristol, there are Michelin starred restaurants in Warsaw now, can you believe that? And as the century turns, jostling for space in the *Stary Rynek*, trying to ignore the cold, Mareczek says he loves her. *'Kocham Cię.'* (*I love you.*)

MARIA: New millennium!

EWA: Another day.

ANNA: *'Kocham Cię.'* (*I love you.*) He says it again.

MARIA: She celebrate at Polish club. In Reading. Is very fun. *śledź* (*herring*) and *Barszcz*. She get tipsy. Mr Baldin. Paweł. He very friendly. He ask her dance. He no want funny funny, and

71

she no want also, just to dance. Very nice man.

EWA: Patrick says this can't go on.

ANNA: And she (*mouthing words*), she wants to say it back.

MARIA: She no want stay so late, she old. They old, all of them.

EWA: She wants to close her eyes.

ANNA: (*Mouths 'Ja Cię kocham.'*)

MARIA: They alive.

EWA: To not be here.

ANNA: (*Continuing to mouth words*)

MARIA: She miss Jerzy. More and more, she missing. One day in garden, her back hurt, she think of him, digging. He like this in garden. Now she like also.

EWA: He says it again.

ANNA: She wants to say it back.

MARIA: But at night. No good.

EWA: And she thinks he's right.

ANNA: And suddenly she's freezing.

MARIA: (*Goes into nightmare*) Wiktor! *Nie, nie, nie!*

EWA: 'No', she says. 'You're right.'

ANNA: It IS freezing. -10, -20. Is anywhere on the planet colder than this?

MARIA: She want forget. All of it.

EWA: Siberia.

ANNA: Siberia!

MARIA: She get up for water. Shaking and... pills. GP give for to sleep. She take. Anything. For to forget.

EWA: Siberia.

MARIA: But she no sleep and... (*Finds mobile, calls Anna*)

ANNA: Babciu?

MARIA: Anna.

ANNA: *Jest bardzo późno, Babciu.* (*It's very late, Babcia.*)

MARIA: *Wiem. Bardzo późno.* (*I know. Very late.*)

ANNA: *Wszystko w porządku?* (*Are you ok?*)

MARIA: *Tak.* (*Yes.*)

ANNA: *Babciu.* Are you ok?

MARIA: *Teraz już tak.* (*I'm ok now.*)

ANNA: What do you mean you're ok now?

MARIA: Now I hear you.

ANNA: *Babciu*, have you taken your pills?

MARIA: Was dream. Bad dream.

ANNA: But you're alright?

MARIA: *Aha. Przepraszam, Anna.* (*Yes, I'm sorry, Anna.*)

ANNA: You don't need to say sorry, I... I'm glad you're alright.

MARIA: *Dobranoc Anna.* (*Goodnight Anna.*)

ANNA: *Dobranoc Babciu.* (*Goodnight Babcia.*) (*Quickly*) *Babciu* – have you told Mama?

MARIA: *O czym?* (*What?*)

ANNA: About the nightmares.

MARIA: *Nie.* (*No.*)

ANNA: It's just she's closer and...

MARIA: (*Interrupts*) She no close.

ANNA: ...she could help you.

MARIA: How she help?

ANNA: I don't know.

MARIA: No one help, Anna. Dreams, they...

ANNA: What?

MARIA: Bad.

ANNA:	What happens in the dreams?
MARIA:	*Nic.* (*Nothing.*)
ANNA:	Nothing? Well something must…
MARIA:	(*interrupts*) Tell me about Warsaw.
ANNA:	What?
MARIA:	About city. What you see? When you go for walk or somesuch.
ANNA:	Well, you know Warsaw, *Babciu*.
MARIA:	I know past. Is all. But dead. They make dead. Everything.
ANNA:	I know.
MARIA:	*No tak.* (*Yeah.*)
ANNA:	But they've rebuilt it, *Babciu*, you know that, the old town and…
MARIA:	*To nie to samo.* (*It's not the same.*)
ANNA:	Some things are the same.
MARIA:	*Niby co?* (*What?*)
ANNA:	Park Łazienkowski. The gardens, and the Chopin concerts.
MARIA:	You do this?
ANNA:	Yeah on Sundays. Everyone goes there.
MARIA:	Is good.

ANNA:	Yeah. *Babciu*, your dreams…
MARIA:	(*Interrupts*) I don't want talk about it.
ANNA:	Ok. It's ok.
MARIA:	*Dziękuję Ci. Kocham Cię Anna.* (*Thank you. I love you Anna*)
ANNA:	*Kocham Cię.* (*I love you.*) And get some sleep now. (*Phone call ends.*)
MARIA:	She miss her.
ANNA:	She misses her.
MARIA:	Very much.
ANNA:	Like it hurts.

(*Pause*)

Then one day Mama comes.

(*Anna's flat in Warsaw. Ewa plumping up cushions, she's just arrived.*)

EWA:	It's er… nice
ANNA:	Yeah.
EWA:	Very spacious.
ANNA:	It's cheap.
EWA:	Could do with a lick of paint, and the skirting boards…
ANNA:	(*Interrupts*) You didn't give me much notice.

EWA:	No, it was… spontaneous. I'd been thinking about it of course. For ages, yes. It was the first thing I thought about when… I'll go and see Anna. That's what I thought. (*Pause*) The pause between thinking and acting that's the thing. The thing that always stops you. Stops me.
ANNA:	Why don't you sit down, Mama?
EWA:	I've been sitting in the cab for ages. The traffic here makes London seem like an Edwardian village.
ANNA:	Yeah, there's lots of congestion, new buildings everywhere and…
EWA:	I couldn't believe the shops. By the station. Gap and H&M and Mango and…
ANNA:	What did you expect?
EWA:	I… I don't know.
ANNA:	It's been 10 years since the Wall, 5 since *Dziadek* (*Pause*) We can go this afternoon if you want?
EWA:	Where?
ANNA:	The grave.
EWA:	No.
ANNA:	When you want.

EWA:	I didn't come for *Dziadek*. I'll visit the grave of course. Absolutely. (*Pause*) I'm here for you and… (*Pause*) I wanted to tell you in person…
ANNA:	Tell me what?
EWA:	Your father.
ANNA:	What about him?
EWA:	It's not something you'd want to put in an email. Not really. (*Pause*) He's left me.
ANNA:	What?
EWA:	I'm sorry.
ANNA:	You mean like…divorce.
EWA:	You don't have to say it!
ANNA:	Fuck!
EWA:	Anna!
ANNA:	Sorry. I'm sorry. About the divorce.
EWA:	Don't be. It's done now. Done and dusted. *Decree Nisi*. I'm a free agent. (*Beat*) Free of him. It's really quite liberating. I wanted to leave him.
ANNA:	Did you?
EWA:	I used to fantasise about it for years. I couldn't quite bring myself to… well, the church for one thing, and then, you…

78

ANNA:	(*Interrupts*) Me?
EWA:	I wanted us to be a family. A proper family.
ANNA:	We were. We are. (*Pause*)
EWA:	Don't you think it's a good thing?
ANNA:	Maybe.
EWA:	I hoped you'd see it as a good thing. I mean divorce is never good of course, it goes against promises made in God's house, but there are circumstances...
ANNA:	He tried, Mama.
EWA:	What?
ANNA:	Dad, it's not like he didn't try.
EWA:	Are you taking his side?
ANNA:	No.
EWA:	I hoped you'd be above taking sides, Anna. That you'd be grown up about it.
ANNA:	I'm not taking sides.
EWA:	But I deserved it, did I?
ANNA:	No.
EWA:	Did I deserve him having an affair?
ANNA:	Mama!

EWA:	A man needs someone, doesn't he? Someone who understands him. (*Pause*) Someone who'll listen in the small hours when the terrors come? (*Pause*) Come home, Anna. (*Pause*) Come back to London. (*Pause*) I say home. It's not really home. I'm in West Hampstead now. I wanted something more central. (*Pause*) He offered to go, but... well, I... it was always his house. His more than mine. I... I was an outsider. There. I felt an outsider.
ANNA:	(*Pause*) I'm not coming back to London.
EWA:	Oh it's big enough. I insisted on a room for you. And there are some pleasing features. High ceilings, a Victorian fireplace. I can show you the particulars, here... (*Gives Anna particulars*)
ANNA:	Yeah, it looks good.
EWA:	Take it!
ANNA:	It's ok, Mama.
EWA:	You can show your boyfriend.
ANNA:	Mareczek?
EWA:	See what he values it at. He can come and stay. Your room has a double bed.
ANNA:	Really?

EWA:	You have these rules and suddenly they don't apply anymore and you have to find different ones. That's what I'm doing. Learning the rules.
ANNA:	Yeah...
EWA:	It's what you have to do. If you're an immigrant.
ANNA:	You're not an immigrant, Mama. You're a British citizen.
EWA:	I tried to belong, Anna. All my life, I've tried. (*Pause*) Now... I've stopped. (*Pause*) Will you come back?
ANNA:	I can't.
EWA:	I've said he can stay.
ANNA:	It's not that simple. We've got jobs here.
EWA:	You're not going to teach TEFL for ever.
ANNA:	No. Maybe...It's what I do now. And Mareczek – there's his business.
EWA:	We're in the digital age. He can still do that. Cheap flights to Warsaw, people commute...
ANNA:	(*Interrupts*) I don't think he'd want to.
EWA:	Have you asked him?
ANNA:	Obviously not.

EWA:	You need to ask him. He's a nice boy, polite, not unintelligent. I get on with him. I think we understand each other.
ANNA:	I don't want to move to London right now. Okay.
EWA:	What about your future?
ANNA:	I'm not thinking about the future.
EWA:	Well, I think you should be.
ANNA:	I'm happy here.
EWA:	Are you?
ANNA:	(*Hesitates*) Yeah.
EWA:	(*Pause*) If you change your mind.
ANNA:	I won't.
EWA:	Please. (*Pause*)
ANNA:	Mum.
EWA:	Come back. I need you to come back. (*Pause*) Anna. (*Pause*) We used to be close.
ANNA:	I used to do what you wanted. (*Pause*)

2.4

2005

The women are in different places as in 2.1 / 2.2

ANNA: She's 30 years old and there is a ring, diamond, 18 carat, on her finger and they are celebrating her birthday with hot chocolate at the *Wawel* café and… and she feels weird. Not because she's 30 or because they've sent out the invitations but just… yeah. (*Pause*) She's busy, not just the teaching, now she helps Mareczek with the admin, showing people round the properties. She mainly does the Westerners, English speakers, often it's other Poles, 2nd generation, 3rd generation, returning not just for financial investment but to reclaim something, a little part of who they are, who they might have been.

MARIA: You can carry something for long time.

ANNA: She does a good sell, Mareczek says. The buyers identify with her Englishness and with her Polish roots. She's perfect, he says. He couldn't have dreamt her up.

MARIA: From one century to new one, from one country to another one, from prison to freedom, from Siberia to Reading.

ANNA: She doesn't want to be perfect.

MARIA: She no more want.

ANNA:	But Mareczek. Mareczek wants to be perfect. He wins an award for entrepreneurial excellence and she goes with him to the ceremony where glamorous women quiz her about shopping in London and she doesn't tell them about Oxfam and clothes swapping parties.
MARIA:	No more carry.
ANNA:	She looks at him. His excitement over profit margins and escalating rents. She thinks there is a new Warsaw and it is him. She thinks I don't like it.
MARIA:	This weight – heavy. Too heavy.
ANNA:	Out of the café window, she sees people begging for prescriptions and she's fiddling in her purse for *złote* and he's getting irritated. 'Don't you get beggars in London?' '*Mamy*,' she says, 'yeah,' but she's not sure that's relevant. 'Your homelessness is out of control,' he says.
MARIA:	No more.
ANNA:	'That's capitalism,' she says. He says, 'You can't have it both ways,' and she knows it's over.
MARIA:	Her life ok now, yes, better. Her daughter, she say, you so different, Mama.

ANNA: In the UK, Dad apologises like it's his fault. He's getting married to Linda and he hopes she'll be ok with it. 'Yeah, she's nice,' she says.

MARIA: Her daughter, she no understand. At night, no good. Bad dreams.

ANNA: Dad wants her to come back now. He says there's nothing left for her in Poland.

MARIA: *Jerzy, co zrobiłeś?* (*What have you done, Jerzy?*)

ANNA: 'Have you seen your mother?' Dad asks? 'Yes,' she says. He says that's good.

MARIA: *Nienawidzę cię!* (*I hate you!*)

ANNA: Then Dad says, 'Sometimes you can't help a patient and that's how it is.'

MARIA: *Nie, nie, nie!* (*No, no, no.*) (*Maria carries on screaming, stops suddenly.*)

ANNA: And she wonders is he talking about Mama or is he talking about me?

(*Pause*)

(*Anna phones Maria*)

MARIA: Anna?

ANNA: Babciu.

MARIA: *Jak sie czujesz* (*How are you?*)

ANNA: I'm fine. I just I… I… how are you *Babciu?*

85

MARIA: I working. In garden. Like always. Digging for to plant...

ANNA: (*Interrupts*) I'm coming home.

MARIA: *Co masz na myśli, mówiąc 'home'? (What do you mean 'home'?)*

ANNA: To the UK.

MARIA: *Aha. Kiedy przyjedziesz? (When will you come?)*

ANNA: I don't know. I'll have to get a ticket and yeah hand in my notice and...

MARIA: *Jesteś chora? (Are you ill?)*

ANNA: No, I'm not ill. I... I've had enough.

MARIA: *Czy nie lubisz już Warszawy? (Don't you like Warsaw anymore?)*

ANNA: I love Warsaw! You know that. It's just... it's time.

MARIA: *Chodzi o chłopca? (Is it the boy?)*

ANNA: Marek. Yeah. Kind of. It's yeah, over.

MARIA: *Co 'over'? (What do you mean 'over'?)*

ANNA: Like I don't love him anymore. Like I never did and... I just want to come home.

MARIA: Anna I happy you coming.

ANNA: Yeah?

MARIA:	*Oczywiście. (Of course.) (Beat)* You tell Ewa?
ANNA:	No. Not yet. She likes Marek and you know what she's like.
MARIA:	Aha.
ANNA:	She'll make it into a huge thing and it's not and…
MARIA:	*(Interrupts)* When you stop to love someone is good to go.
ANNA:	Yeah. Thanks.
MARIA:	Otherwise dead. Marriage dead.
ANNA:	I'm not married.
MARIA:	And life nothing.
ANNA:	Are you talking about Mama?
MARIA:	My life.
ANNA:	*Babciu…*
MARIA:	*(Pause)* I happy you coming.

(Pause)

EWA:	She didn't have to get a job. The divorce settlement was generous. Patrick has always been generous. He likes to do things properly, fairly. *(Pause)* She didn't expect to like it. She hadn't even taught primary before but it's a private school, small classes and the children are happy. She thinks, she feels… this is not

happiness but... satisfaction. (*Beat*) Satisfaction and not satisfaction. Because she still... Wiktor... she doesn't think about him every day. No, no she does. She thinks about him every day but not every hour, every minute, every second. She can think about other things. She wants to. To think about other things. She wants to be free. And... and... and...

(*Pause*)

And one day she finds herself on a plane to Siberia. *Nowy Sibersk*. It's late Spring, warm, and as she catches a first glimpse of the landscape, the flatness... she remembers nothing.

(*Pause*)

There's no grave. She wasn't expecting a grave, but... something.

(*Pause*)

MEMORY: Siberia, March 1942

MARIA: Siberia. March 1942. 'I no go. I no leave Siberia.' She tell him this many times, but he no listen.

'We free now!' he say. 'Free! *Wolni!*' (*Free*). Where you want go, Jerzy? 'You want stay here?' He say.

'I no leave my son,' she say.

'Your son dead,' he say.

'He here,' she say.

'Where?' he ask her.

'Where? Where? *Gdzie? Gdzie? Gdzie? (Where? Where? Where?)* Show me where!'

And she look... She look.

(*Pause*)

They put him in snow. All babies in snow.

(*Pause*)

Ewa... she asking... after '*Gdzie jest Wiktor, Tatuś?*' (*Where is Wiktor, Tatuś?*)

'Wiktor in snow now,' he answer, and Ewa, she say, *Jak płatek śniegu. (Like a snowflake.)* Like a snowflake.

And she think, yes. *Jak płatek śniegu. (Like a snowflake)* Cold and light and fragile and silent.

(*Pause*)

But now Spring. Soon will be no more snow and outside is truck and Jerzy, he impatient. 'Maria. We go now. We lucky - we have lift. We will go South, join Army, leave Russia...'

'I no want leave,' she say.

'And we eat,' he say. 'Again will be food.'

'*Nie (no)*', she say.

'Maria, you will die here.'

She think she dead already. '*Nie obchodzi mnie to!*' (*I don't care.*) I don't care.

'*Maria, proszę! Pomyśl o Ewie!*' (*Please! Think of Ewa!*)

EWA:　　She walks and cries and there's a smell... she can't place it. Something earthy in the air and...and she thinks of her father. His arms, strong arms, holding her.

MARIA:　　Ewa. In his arms she very little. She think, Ewa, she no come to me now. For milk yes, but is all. (*Pause*) 'I stay here,' she say.

EWA:　　She thinks of the places they went to from here, crossing countries, continents, Iran, Africa... She no longer knows what's story, what's memory, what's invention, but his arms, holding her, carrying her, loving her. What did he go through to keep her safe? How do you build a life after...? How do you love? (*Pause*)

MARIA:　　Jerzy, he put down Ewa. He pick her up. He weak also, *oczywiście*, (*Of course*), of course everyone weak but she skeleton and Ewa, she crying now, '*Tatuśiu! Tatuśiu!*'

EWA:　　She came to find Wiktor but she's missing *Tatuś*. (*Pause*)

MARIA: And she want scream: put me down! *Put me down!* (*Opens her mouth, trying to scream, pause*) but is nothing. (*Pause*) Jerzy, he carry her to truck, she no scream but she kick, hard, with leg, and other men, they are helping him and inside are other people men, women, children – she no look at them.

EWA: She can't remember Wiktor, she thought she... here... she hoped... but she can't remember him and that's... that's how it is. But *Tatuś* (*as if speaking directly to her father*) '*Tatuśiu!*'

MARIA: Now she scream. Wiktor! Wiktor!

EWA: '*Tatuśiu! Tatuśiu!*'

2.5

HEATHROW, AUGUST 2005 /

LIVERPOOL DOCKS, AUGUST 1946

Anna and Maria in separate spaces.

MARIA:	Liverpool.
ANNA:	London.
MARIA:	August 1946.
ANNA:	August 2005.
MARIA:	Another place.
ANNA:	She's back.
MARIA:	She think of all places she has been.
ANNA:	She thinks of Warsaw.
MARIA:	It is enough now she think.
ANNA:	She thinks that nothing is certain and how much time we waste trying to pretend otherwise.
MARIA:	Ewa, she take her hand as they walk down steps.
ANNA:	She drives to Reading.
MARIA:	For her is exciting, new place.
ANNA:	To *Babcia*'s bungalow. It makes her feel safe.

MARIA:	And she talking, she many questions. 'Can we see Buckingham Palace today?' 'Can we have fish and chip for tea?'
ANNA:	*Babcia* has hundreds of questions as usual.
MARIA:	And Jerzy, Ewa, she looking for him all time. She tell her many times he come later, not now, Ewunia, but still she looking. '*Tatuś*, *Tatuś*?'
ANNA:	And she wants to know about Marek but she can't explain.
(*Pause*)	
MARIA:	They wait for bus to resettlement camp.
ANNA:	Later, on the way back to London, she gets stuck on the M25.
MARIA:	And wait and wait.
ANNA:	And she's sick of waiting and suddenly she's crying and she doesn't know why. It's just cars.
MARIA:	She cold.
ANNA:	It looks miserable outside.
MARIA:	She think in Poland can be also in August cold. Is possible.
ANNA:	She wonders if it's hot in Warsaw, but so what, she's here now.

MARIA:	She remember cold in Siberia.
ANNA:	She wonders what she'll do now.
MARIA:	She no want remember this. This England she think. This somewhere else. This somewhere for to make new memories.
ANNA:	Go back to uni. Get a job.
MARIA:	She no want go from here somewhere else. She want put past behind her.
ANNA:	It'll be fine and if not, well, she can go back to Warsaw.
MARIA:	She want be warm, have food, work. She want survive.
ANNA:	Yeah.
MARIA:	And forget.

(*Anna arrives at Ewa's London flat. Takes out key, hesitates, rings bell*)

EWA:	Anna.
ANNA:	Mama.
EWA:	(*Hugs Anna fiercely*)
ANNA:	Mama are you?
EWA:	You're here.
ANNA:	Yeah. Mama have you been drinking?
EWA:	I'm happy to have you back and alive…

ANNA: Yeah.

EWA: *Welcome home, darling!* Welcome home!

ANNA: Home.

Act Three

2015 – 2016

3.1

NOVEMBER 2015.

Maria is in her bedroom in Ewa's West Hampstead flat. Smartly dressed. Looks impatiently at watch. Ewa is in her bedroom next door. Anna is in her bedroom in North London house she rents with boyfriend.

MARIA:	Today big day!
ANNA:	Today she doesn't want to get out of bed.
EWA:	40! Her daughter!
MARIA:	*Moja Kochana Anna!* (*My darling Anna!*)
ANNA:	It's not like her. She's always on the go. And… yeah. Maybe she's been overdoing it.
EWA:	It's 2015.
MARIA:	(*Sudden pain in head*) *Nie, znowu!* (*Not again!*) Today she want ok.
ANNA:	Work and Simon and yeah…
EWA:	She wants today to go smoothly.
MARIA:	Today she want see.
ANNA:	She's got no energy.
EWA:	But it's tricky with Mama. She's so particular about everything. Food and clothes and her

room, and especially where Anna's concerned. Everything has to be perfect for Anna.

MARIA: (*Recurrence of pain*) Ah, is no good. *Zostaw mnie!* (*Go away!*) (*Shuts her eyes, breathes*)

ANNA: Fuck it!

EWA: And then there's her headaches.

MARIA: Some day ok.

ANNA: She phones Mama and says she's sorry but she's not feeling well.

MARIA: Some day no ok.

ANNA: And she needs to postpone the party.

EWA: She tells Anna she understands and worries how to break the news to Mama.

MARIA: She no understand. Anna, she very healthy. What this illness? Some flu or somesuch?

ANNA: She hears the disappointment in Mama's voice.

EWA: She hears the disappointment in Mama's voice and tells her that it's some sort of sick bug and that's the last thing they want.

MARIA: She tell Ewa sick bug nothing.

ANNA: It's probably nothing really, just... exhaustion, yeah.

EWA: Mama is being difficult.

MARIA:	*Moja Anna!* (*My Anna!*)
ANNA:	And she's behind on her translation deadline and there's some problem with Simon's daughter and his ex is stressing him out as usual and...
MARIA:	He no good for Anna this Simon.
EWA:	Mama blames Simon of course.
ANNA:	Simon wants her to go to the Doctors because he's so worried about her.
MARIA:	Divorced man. No good.
EWA:	Just because he's divorced.
ANNA:	But he still takes his daughter to gymnastics.
MARIA:	Ewa, she no understand what this mean, to her. This party. Anna party. For months she waiting. And all morning she getting ready.
ANNA:	But that's fine.
EWA:	'It's fine.' She tries to reassure Mama. 'Anna will rearrange it, Mama. Next week.'
ANNA:	She's his daughter.
MARIA:	Next week she may be dead.
EWA:	Mama exaggerates and criticises the new dress she specially bought for the occasion.
MARIA:	Ewa dress – terrible!

ANNA:	Simon says she looks terrible.
EWA:	She tells Mama it's not her fault that the party is cancelled.
MARIA:	Green no good colour for her, no.
ANNA:	She wonders if they'll stay together. She hasn't wondered this before. They just are and they get on with it, and the years stack up and her Polish is still pretty fluent, well it has to be for work but that's good because…it matters. And sometimes she corrects *Babcia*.
EWA:	And it is not her fault Anna is ill.
MARIA:	She tell Ewa she no make Anna happy.
ANNA:	She wonders if they could be happy? (*quickly*) They are happy but… could they… could she…?
EWA:	Mama is tiring and needs her nap.
MARIA:	She tell Ewa she no good mother.
EWA:	She wants to slap Mama in the face.
ANNA:	Could she be happy?
MARIA:	Anna she 40, she no husband, she no happy.
EWA:	She tells Mama of course Anna is happy and *she* hasn't exactly set the bar high. She tells Mama that she's been asleep all her life and she knows nothing.

MARIA:	She know many things. Hunger. Fear. Hurt. Guilt.
ANNA:	She just doesn't know.
EWA:	Nothing!
MARIA:	She say nothing. 'Go, Ewa, please!'
ANNA:	No.

3.2

2015

Ewa's living room, about six weeks later. Early evening.

Loud knocking on door. Ewa answers.

EWA:	Anna...?
ANNA:	(*Shivering and distressed*) Can I come in?
EWA:	Yes, of course, *Kochanie* (*Darling*). Just be quiet, we don't want to wake *Babcia*.
ANNA:	Is she asleep?
EWA:	Yes, she's been waking up at night this week, so she settles down early. What are you doing out in this weather? You're soaked. Did I miss a text? I thought we said Sunday. Anna?
ANNA:	I don't know.
EWA:	Are you alright?
ANNA:	No.
EWA:	Well, sit down, and take those things off. Can I get you anything?
ANNA:	Water.
EWA:	You look like you need a vodka tonic.
ANNA:	No.
EWA:	At least have a cup of tea to warm you up. Here (*Passing water*) I'll put the kettle on.

ANNA: I'm pregnant, Mum.

EWA: What?

ANNA: Yeah.

EWA: Goodness, Anna. Are you sure?

ANNA: Yeah.

EWA: I can't... I can't believe I'm hearing this. I
           think I need a drink. I expect you need one
           too?

ANNA: It makes me sick.

EWA: Yes, you're looking peaky. Well, that's to be
           expected.

ANNA: I feel so sick.

EWA: That's not a bad sign. How many weeks...?

ANNA: 12.

EWA: Three months! (*Beat*) You didn't tell me...

ANNA: No.

EWA: Well, you're out of the danger zone as they
           say. It's really happening.

ANNA: I don't know.

EWA: But you've had a scan?

ANNA: Yeah.

EWA: And...?

ANNA:	It was fine.
EWA:	Well, that's a relief. At your age, there are risks...
ANNA:	I thought I'd have a miscarriage. Because I didn't realise at first, I'd been drinking, you know my birthday, and Simon smokes in the house...
EWA:	You can relax now. Once you've had the scan, it's...
ANNA:	I wanted to miscarry.
EWA:	What?
ANNA:	I hoped I would. If you're 40 there's a 50 % chance...
EWA:	Don't talk like this!
ANNA:	I don't want it, Mum.
EWA:	You're shocked, darling.
ANNA:	I don't sleep.
EWA:	That will be your hormones. You need to give it a few weeks, be kind to yourself, rest. I know it wasn't part of your plan, I'd quite ruled out the Grandma thing.
ANNA:	Please!
EWA:	I'm not complaining – that was your choice.
ANNA:	I can't go through with it.

EWA:	I'll help you.
ANNA:	No.
EWA:	And I'm sure he'll want to marry you now.
ANNA:	What?
EWA:	Simon.
ANNA:	Are you joking?
EWA:	You've lived with him for four years now, it's about time you settled down.
ANNA:	We're fine as we are.
EWA:	Yes, but with the pregnancy...
ANNA:	And I think you'd be the last person who'd be advocating marriage.
EWA:	What?
ANNA:	Sorry, I didn't mean... I...
EWA:	You're right.
ANNA:	No, I'm... I'm all over the place and I feel so sick. The last few weeks it's been one deadline after another and... I'm tired.

(*Pause*)

EWA:	With your father, sometimes I think I'm completely over it and other times I'm not.
ANNA:	I'm going to get a termination, mum.

EWA:	What?
ANNA:	I should have done it earlier. I didn't think I'd get this far.
EWA:	You are... no... you can't.
ANNA:	Why...?
EWA:	Because it's against God's will. Because there is a living creature inside of you who deserves a life.
ANNA:	That's your opinion.
EWA:	It's the truth.
ANNA:	Shut up! (*Putting her coat back on*) I wasn't going to tell you.
EWA:	So why are you here?
ANNA:	Yeah, I didn't plan it, coming here. I was just walking and walking and...
EWA:	Why are you even telling me if you've made up your mind?
ANNA:	I... I don't know.
EWA:	You could have just gone ahead, booked the abortion, you know...
ANNA:	I couldn't. That's the thing. I can't. (*Pause*) I can't.
EWA:	Sit down, *Kochanie* (*Pause*) Look, it's raining out there, you can't go out in this.

ANNA:	(*Sits down, pause*)
EWA:	Do you know how long I waited for you?
ANNA:	Yeah.
EWA:	Ten years. They couldn't explain it. Why it didn't happen before? Do you know what that does to a marriage?
ANNA:	This is not about you, Mama.
EWA:	It kills it.
ANNA:	You can't blame me for that.
EWA:	Waiting and waiting and tests and more tests and hope and disappointment and miscarriages...
ANNA:	You had...
EWA:	One after the other, after the other, after the other...
ANNA:	I didn't...
EWA:	No. (*Pause*) How much I wanted you. (*Pause*) When I held you...
ANNA:	Mama, please.
EWA:	I want you to feel that, when you hold your baby.
ANNA:	(*Pause*) I'm scared.
EWA:	You've had the scan...

ANNA:	A thousand things can go wrong.
EWA:	That's life, you have to give it to God.
ANNA:	Like you did?
EWA:	No, I failed. But you don't need to.
ANNA:	I'm so scared. I can't live like this for another 6 months. And... what if it dies?
EWA:	Why would it die?
ANNA:	I don't know.
EWA:	I'll help you.
ANNA:	How...?
EWA:	Let me. (*Ewa takes Anna's hands. Pause*)
ANNA:	What will *Babcia* say?
EWA:	She'll be happy because... because it's you.
ANNA:	Are you sure?
EWA:	Or if not, it'll all be my fault.
ANNA:	No it won't. (*Pause*) What if I go ahead? (*Pause*) With the termination?
(*Pause*)	
EWA:	When I went to Siberia...
ANNA:	What?
EWA:	Do you remember?

ANNA:	Yeah but that's like 10 years ago.
EWA:	I said goodbye to *Tatuś*. (*Beat*) And to Wiktor.
ANNA:	Mum please. Do not do a guilt trip on me!
EWA:	No, no, no. I let Wiktor go, Anna. Do you see?
ANNA:	No.
EWA:	But you, you're here. (*Pause*) I don't want to lose you.
ANNA:	If I go ahead…?
EWA:	You don't need my permission.
ANNA:	Thanks.

(*They hug one another*)

3.3

2015.

Maria's bedroom.

MEMORY

MARIA: Siberia. March 1941.

(*Pause*)

She sick very often. She think is nothing. Everyone sick here.

(*Pause*)

One day she digging, in quarry, like always. Winter will be soon, but today warm and no wind and she hot. Very hot. She stop. (*Panting*) Is no good stop because guard he will see, but she no help this. For one minute she stop and... and someone give water. (*Drinking water*) *Bardzo Ci dziękuję.* (*Thank you very much.*) (*Spits out water*) Metal, in mouth, taste is metal. (*Beat*) She know this taste. From no vitamin, say other women, but she know.

(*Pause*)

In camp is woman. Midwife. She know what to do, but she want money. (*Beat*) In shoe she have cross, very small, but silver, Mother Jerzy, she give for wedding.

(*Pause*)

After, she think she dying. After, he hit her. Before never and after never, but this time – he angry. She wait for bleeding. Woman she say two days but nothing. She whisper to woman, 'How much longer?' Woman, she no sure. 'Is everyone different.' She wait and wait. And soon her belly bigger. One day she feel kicking and... she happy. Jerzy, he sorry he angry. He say, 'If God want,' but she think there is no God here. No.

3.4

2016

Summer. Anna's house, nursery.

Anna is obsessively cleaning a cot in nursery. Ewa watches her.

EWA:	The cot looks lovely. (*Pause*) You've made a good choice. (*Pause*) I don't think you need to clean it quite so vigorously.
ANNA:	Germs.
EWA:	It's brand new, yes?
ANNA:	Packaging! The factory.
EWA:	*Kochanie*, I'm sure those wipes are full of nasty chemicals and...
ANNA:	Shit!
EWA:	Anna!
ANNA:	(*Dropping wipes, looking at her hands in panic*) I didn't think... I'd better wash my hands. You can get organic ones. I'll order some. (*Looking on phone*)
EWA:	I didn't mean...
ANNA:	These look good. Free of carbon...
EWA:	Why don't you sit down a minute?
ANNA:	I don't know what mattress to buy?

EWA:	One that fits a cot. I expect they're all a standard size.
ANNA:	Some can cause cot death.
EWA:	What?
ANNA:	And you can't reuse them.
EWA:	You're a getting a new one?
ANNA:	What about the fibres?
EWA:	Darling, you seem very anxious about this.
ANNA:	Yeah I've read up on it.
EWA:	You just need a new mattress and it'll be absolutely fine.
ANNA:	I have to get this right.
EWA:	Why don't I order it for you?
ANNA:	No.
EWA:	I could help you choose which one.
ANNA:	You don't get it.
EWA:	Anna…
ANNA:	If it died.
EWA:	Anna! You're… look, what sort of a mattress do you think I slept on for heaven's sake?
ANNA:	I can't.

112

EWA:	Sweetheart!
ANNA:	I'm scared. Is everyone scared?
EWA:	Yes, up to a point.
ANNA:	Are they?
EWA:	Yes but...
ANNA:	I don't know what to do.
EWA:	I think we should start by seeing a doctor.
ANNA:	I can't go to the surgery.
EWA:	If I call now, we might still get an afternoon...
ANNA:	No.
EWA:	He could prescribe something to help you sleep.
ANNA:	Medication. Chemicals. That could fuck the baby's brain.
EWA:	Be reasonable!
ANNA:	There are germs at the surgery, chicken pox, toxoplasmosis... I want him to live. (*She curls up in the floor, Ewa runs to her, strokes her*)
MARIA:	(*In separate space to Ewa and Anna, cradling a baby*) I want he live.
ANNA:	(*Still on floor with Ewa*) I'm scared.
MARIA:	But how...? Here.

ANNA:	Mama.
MARIA:	I want hold him.
ANNA:	It could die.
MARIA:	I want hold and no let go.
ANNA:	No.
MARIA:	When they take him, he breathing. He very sick. But he breathe.
ANNA:	(*Trying to breathe calmly*)
MARIA:	He still alive, but I... I dead.
ANNA:	(*She has gone to sleep. Maria walks over to her and touches her.*)

3.5

MEMORY

ANNA:	1983. I'm eight and it's summer and I'm at *Dziadek's* house in Reading.
EWA:	1983 and we're visiting *Tatuś* and Mama, and in Poland there is still Martial Law.
MARIA:	1983. I tired and I no care about Poland.
ANNA:	*Dziadek* takes me outside and I'm riding on his shoulders in the garden.
EWA:	I watch them in the garden.
MARIA:	I watch them in garden.
ANNA:	And I'm so high I am screaming!
EWA:	I'm horrified that her screaming could upset the neighbours.
MARIA:	Screaming too loud!
ANNA:	And *Dziadek* twirls me round and round and I could fall off but I don't because he's squeezing my ankles so tightly that I say, '*Dziadek* stop that!', but I feel safe.
EWA:	And I'm thinking is she safe?
MARIA:	And I thinking now I getting headache.
ANNA:	And tall. I mean really tall like I'm Jack and I've just climbed to the top of the beanstalk

	but I'm a girl so I can't be Jack but I could be Rapunzel in her tower.
EWA:	I need to keep her safe.
MARIA:	But she need play. Children need play.
ANNA:	And I can see everything. For miles. I can see the whole world. London – that's where we live, and Poland.
EWA:	I stop looking at them to calm down and I try to talk to Mama about Poland.
MARIA:	I no want talk about Poland.
EWA:	What's it like when you can't go out in the evenings?
MARIA:	I no like go out.
ANNA:	And then in the garden *Dziadek* pretends he's going to drop me.
EWA:	I'm worried he's going to drop her.
MARIA:	He no drop her.
ANNA:	And I pretend to fall.
EWA:	That she'll have a bad fall.
MARIA:	And I thinking of Ewa. When she little. How he play with her also.
ANNA:	And *Dziadek* laughs and says, '*Zupełnie jak Mama*' (*Just like Mama*) which means I'm just like Mama. But that's a lie because I'm

116

not like Mama at all because she never laughs
because she's too worried about headlice and
eating all your greens up.

EWA: And Patrick will say I've been neglecting her,
                but where is he when I need him?

MARIA: I think for Jerzy easy. Very easy. To play and
                some such. To be father.

ANNA: So I tell *Dziadek* I'm not like Mama but he
                says, 'All girls are the same.' And then I ask
                him about *Babcia*. Did she go on his shoulders
                too? And now he's laughing and I'm laughing
                too...

EWA: Now they're laughing...

ANNA: ...and I wish...

EWA: I wish I didn't worry so much.

MARIA: I wish this can be different.

ANNA: I wish *Dziadek* could live with us forever
                because he plays the best games and Dad's
                too busy.

EWA: And that Patrick would play with her.

MARIA: Different with Jerzy. (*beat*) With me.

ANNA: Then I ask *Dziadek* a question. 'Why is
                Babcia sad?' He goes quiet and I can't look at
                him because you're not allowed to ask that
                question. No one says you're not allowed but
                you're not.

117

EWA:	But I can't say anything. To Patrick. No.
MARIA:	I wish I can be different.
ANNA:	*Dziadek* puts me down on the grass and his face goes shut and my face goes red like I've done something bad but I haven't.
EWA:	They've stopped the rough and tumble and I think it looks nice outside.
MARIA:	And I want be outside. With Jerzy. With Anna. In garden also.
ANNA:	Then he says, 'You know why, *Malutka*.' And he tells me the story about how the war made *Babcia* sad and he's right – I know this story like I've always known it. All my life. I know about Stalin knocking on the door in the night and going to a camp in Siberia where it's freezing, I know about Mama going to an orphanage in Iran. I know about eating butterflies in the forest and mixing sand with water so your belly is tricked and thinks it's full. I know all this... But... suddenly this story... this story... suddenly I don't understand, and I say, 'But you're not sad, *Dziadek*?'
EWA:	And I feel sad, and silly.
MARIA:	To be happy, hold her hand, pick her up.
EWA:	Silly that I was worried because she'll always be safe with *Tatuś*.

ANNA:	*Dziadek* says, '*Nie.*' (*No.*) Then he says, '*Zapytaj ją, Mała.*' (*You ask her, little one.*) He says I can ask her.
MARIA:	Tell her stories.
EWA:	Like I was.
ANNA:	Why can't you tell me? I say. He says, '*Bo nie wiem.*' (*Because I don't know.*) Because he doesn't know. But I think that's stupid because if you're married to someone you know everything about them, you even sleep in the same bed. But he looks at me and I think... he's telling the truth.
MARIA:	But I can't. *Nie.* (*No.*)
ANNA:	So I get up from the grass and I run into the bungalow.
EWA:	'Take your shoes off, *Malutka.*'
MARIA:	And now she coming in house. Running.
ANNA:	And I forget to take off my shoes.
EWA:	She always forgets to take off her shoes but the carpet is beige and I don't want it getting stained for Mama.
MARIA:	She come to me. *Tak.* (*Yes*). She look at me ` with big eyes.
ANNA:	And I go up to *Babcia*...

119

EWA:	I ask Anna what's wrong. *Coś się stało, Anna?* (*What's wrong Anna?*)
MARIA:	And I think this child, *Moja Anna* (*My Anna*), she will be ok. There is no war, father have good job, Ewa she look after. Is food, money, school.
ANNA:	And I open my mouth...
EWA:	But Anna is not looking at me. She's looking at *Babcia*. They look at each other and... and there's this silence in the rom.
MARIA:	I think is enough.
ANNA:	Then I shut it...
EWA:	It's as if you can feel it, touch it, taste it in your mouth even...
MARIA:	Then I think there is something I want to tell to her.
ANNA:	And I don't say anything.
EWA:	And this silence... when I was a child... it's the same.
MARIA:	I don't know what it is.
ANNA:	I'm just silent.

(*The women look around the room, look at each other.*)

3.6

AUGUST 2016

Afternoon.

Maria has her back to the door. Anna and Ewa enter with Baby Wiktor in a Moses basket.

ANNA: *Babcia!*

MARIA: Anna!

(They hug one another while Ewa puts the sleeping Wiktor down.)

ANNA: It's so good to see you.

MARIA: *Kochana! Moja Kochana! (Darling! My darling!)*

ANNA: I'm afraid he's asleep.

EWA: He always sleeps in the afternoons

MARIA: *Tęskniłam za tobą. (I've missed you.)*

ANNA: I've missed you too, *Babcia*, but I'm ok now.

EWA: You're doing brilliantly, darling.

ANNA: Mama! *(To Maria)* You're going to love him.

EWA: He's dead to the world.

ANNA: Shall we wake him up?

MARIA: *Nie. (No.)*

EWA: It might be best not to disturb his routine.

121

ANNA:	Yeah. I just want to show him off.
EWA:	(*To Wiktor*) You're such a good sleeper.
MARIA:	(*Looks at Wiktor for a long time. Looks away*) You sleep also, *Ewunia*.
EWA:	Really?
MARIA:	I lucky. In wagon is other baby.
EWA:	What do you mean, Mama?
MARIA:	On way to Siberia. You sleep and feed and sleep. For me no problem. But other baby. In wagon. Crying and crying and crying.
EWA:	Mama, let's not get upset, you'll wake him up.
MARIA:	Russian guard, he tired, he no like crying. He say to baby mother, 'Shut up! You shut it up!' He push her, hard and she shake. (*Pause*) You no answer Russian back. Never. But this woman, she answer back. 'Tell me how and I do it!' And baby crying, still crying. Then he shoot, Russian guard, he shoot baby in head.
EWA:	No.
MARIA:	Then is silence. In wagon. Everyone. (*To Ewa*) And you no cry.
ANNA:	I can't hear this.
MARIA:	Baby mother she no cry. And I say nothing. To her. (*Beat, to Ewa*) I want keep you alive. (*Pause*) We lucky now, we safe.

122

ANNA:	Are we?
EWA:	Anna…?
ANNA:	When I'm feeding at night, I'm watching the news and… it's like they hate us again.
MARIA:	Who hate?
ANNA:	Everyone.
EWA:	No one, Mama. (*To Anna*) Anna, you're overreacting… that's natural of course. You're breastfeeding – overemotional.
ANNA:	What?
EWA:	There are always tensions between communities. And not in front of her.
MARIA:	*Co?* (*What?*)
EWA:	It's nothing, Mama.
ANNA:	Nothing?!!
EWA:	Darling it's not as if you're even properly Polish.
ANNA:	What am I then? Who am I?
EWA:	You're half Polish, yes, but you were born here. You're second generation?
ANNA:	So my Polishness doesn't count?
EWA:	So you don't need to worry! I'm trying to reassure you.

ANNA: (*To Ewa*) Sorry. I know, I know, it's just at night, I… it's like I'm waiting for something. Like a knock on the door or a brick to go through the window or…

EWA: (*Interrupts*) Darling, that won't happen.

ANNA: Won't it?

MARIA: One day.

ANNA: One day what?

EWA: She's thinking of something else.

ANNA: No she's not. Nationalism, it's on the rise, everywhere. Don't you watch the news, Mama?

EWA: I try to avoid it. (*Wiktor wakes*) Ah, at last, Wiktor's waking up. Shall I…?

ANNA: I'll get him. Are you ready to hold him now, *Babcia*? (*She cradles Wiktor, about to pass him to Maria*)

MARIA: *Nie.* (*No.*)

EWA: It's alright, Mama, you won't drop him.

MARIA: *Nie chcę go trzymać.* (*I don't want to hold him.*)

ANNA: Why not?

MARIA: Why you calling Wiktor?

ANNA: Because… it's a Polish name, and… you know why, *Babcia*, so that Wiktor is…

EWA:	Why don't you get comfortable, Mama?
MARIA:	*Nie.* (*No.*)
ANNA:	He'd love a cuddle.
MARIA:	I no want.
ANNA:	Why is she so…?
EWA:	I don't know. Maybe she's getting tired. Mama, what's the problem?
MARIA:	*Nic!* (*Nothing!*)
ANNA:	Maybe the name was a bad idea.
MARIA:	I want be alone now.
ANNA:	She doesn't have to hold him, it's…
EWA:	Mama, Anna has brought her new baby, your great grandson, to see you and you're not interested?
MARIA:	*Proszę idźie!* (*Please go!*)
EWA:	Why don't you want to hold him?
ANNA:	Let's leave it, Mama.
EWA:	I am not leaving it.
ANNA:	She's got all upset and…
EWA:	Tell me why you refuse to hold him?
MARIA:	He… your dead brother.

EWA:	Don't be ridiculous. This is not Wiktor.
ANNA:	She's confused. The name…
EWA:	What, she believes in reincarnation now?
ANNA:	Mama, leave it.
EWA:	I want to know why she's behaving like this.
MARIA:	Your dead brother.
EWA:	This is your great grandson, Mama.
MARIA:	Who you killed.
EWA:	What?
ANNA:	She's lost it.
EWA:	Mama, what do you mean?
MARIA:	He die and you live.
EWA:	So that's my fault?
MARIA:	Your father.
EWA:	*Tatuś's* fault?
MARIA:	He no choose Wiktor.
ANNA:	She's not making sense.
EWA:	Wait! What do you mean, Mama?
MARIA:	He ill, Wiktor, and I ill and you ill.
ANNA:	No one's ill now, Babcia.

EWA:	*Cicho, Anna!* (*Be quiet Anna!*)
MARIA:	Is Winter, everyone cough, fever. But my milk still coming. (*Pause*) But Wiktor, he no suck so good, and when he suck, he sick. Jerzy, he say is too late, for Wiktor. We can do nothing, he say.
ANNA:	I don't want to hear this.
EWA:	Listen!
MARIA:	(*To Ewa*) But you, you bigger. Jerzy, he say if I stop feed Wiktor, will be for you milk, and you live. (*Pause*) But Wiktor he want. And I want Wiktor. I no want choose. (*Pause, to Ewa*) Jerzy, he love you, and he take Wiktor from me. (*Pause*) I let him do this. But after, I hate him. Your father. (*Pause*) At first, I no want look at you. Before, when Russian guard shoot other baby, I happy you alive, but after Wiktor, no. I no care. No for Jerzy, no for you, no for me. (*Pause*)
ANNA:	Oh *Babcia!*
EWA:	He died because of me.
ANNA:	No.
EWA:	Yes, that's what she said, that's why... all of it.
ANNA:	Mama, he'd have died anyway. That's what she said.

MARIA: Is true. I no want choose. Ewunia...

EWA: I went to Siberia to find him, but I couldn't, but there... it was so vast and I could imagine it – the snow, the hunger, the desperation and I... I lost something. That feeling... The guilt...

ANNA: It's ok, Mama.

MARIA: After Wiktor... Jerzy... he want make alright. He want I smile. He want again love. Love he say will again be possible.

EWA: But it wasn't.

MARIA: *Nie.* (*No*) (*Pause*) Because I dead. Inside I dead. (*Pause*) but you. With you, he happy. He want you always close to him, very close.

EWA: Yes.

MARIA: *Przepraszam.* (*I'm sorry.*) (*Maria and Ewa look at one another. Pause*)

ANNA: (*To Maria*) Do you want to hold him now?

MARIA: (*Anna gives Wiktor to Maria*) *Cześć maleńki. Wiktor. Mój Wiktor.* (*Hello, little one! Wiktor. My Wiktor.*) *Jesteś piękny.* (*You're beautiful!*) (*Pause*) Is good you here, Wiktor. Very good.

ANNA: I still have to blink.

MARIA: (*To Wiktor*) For you will be different.

ANNA: Yeah, I'll do my best.

MARIA:	Different world.
EWA:	Maybe.
ANNA:	Maybe.

END